Science Frontiers

Developing Your English with National Geographic

Keiko Hattori / Toshio Hidaka / Yayoi Yamashita
Kana Matsuda / Judy Noguchi

Australia • Brazil • Japan • Korea • Mexico • Singapore • Spain • United Kingdom • United States

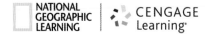

Science Frontiers
—Developing Your English with National Geographic

Keiko Hattori / Toshio Hidaka / Yayoi Yamashita / Kana Matsuda / Judy Noguchi

Associate Manager, Publishing: Tsuyoshi Yoshida

Cover Designer: Naomi Morimura, Creators Union

Text Designer: SEIN

Compositor: SEIN

Photo credits appear on page 104, which constitutes a continuation of the copyright page.

© 2016 National Geographic Learning, a part of Cengage Learning

ALL RIGHTS RESERVED. No part of this work covered by the copyright herein may be reproduced, transmitted, stored or used in any form or by any means graphic, electronic, or mechanical, including but not limited to photocopying, recording, scanning, digitizing, taping, Web distribution, information networks, or information storage and retrieval systems, except as permitted under Section 107 or 108 of the 1976 United States Copyright Act, without the prior written permission of the publisher.

> For permission to use material from this text or product, submit all requests online at www.cengage.com/permissions
> Further permissions questions can be emailed to permissionrequest@cengage.com

For Sale in Japan Only

ISBN: 978-4-86312-289-5

Adapted from the following articles in the following issues of *National Geographic Explorer Pioneer Edition* published by National Geographic Learning, a part of Cengage Learning © 2011, 2012, 2013, 2014 Cengage Learning®

March 2011: Mummy Mystery	
September 2012: Bare Bones	9781285492025
October 2012: The Hidden Lives of Leaves	9781285492049
March 2013: Weirdest Wonders	9781285492100
April 2013: Getting the Shot	9781285492124
September 2013: Into the Rain Forest, Aquarius	9781285958309
October 2013: The Skin You're In	9781285958323
November–December 2013: Turn Up the Heat, Attack of the Germs	9781285958347
January–February 2014: Mission to Mars	9781285958361
March 2014: Free Fall	9781285958385
April 2014: Feed the World	9781285958408
September 2014: Swim the Seahorses, Just Like the Earth	9781305471955

National Geographic Learning
20 Channel Center Street
Boston, MA 02210
USA

Cengage Learning is a leading provider of customized learning solutions with office locations around the globe, including Singapore, the United Kingdom, Australia, Mexico, Brazil, and Japan. Locate your local office at:
international.cengage.com/region

Cengage Learning products are represented in Canada by Nelson Education, Ltd.

Visit **National Geographic Learning** online at ngl.cengage.com

Visit our corporate website at www.cengage.com

はしがき

　本テキストは、『National Geographic Explorer』という科学系雑誌の掲載記事を用いた英語総合教材です。サメやタツノオトシゴなどの生物を題材としたものから、スカイダイビングや火山、惑星に至るまで、幅広い内容を網羅しています。教養として知っておきたい一般的な自然科学系のトピックが扱われていますので、理系・文系の専攻を問わず、幅広くさまざまな興味を持つ学生に役立つ教材です。

　文章読解を学習活動の核にしていますが、語彙確認やトピックに関連した簡単なリスニング、および音読を行ってから本文読解に取り組むという仕組みになっています。また、口頭練習を含めた文法・語法演習による基礎の定着を目指した活動、まとめのリスニングによる内容確認、口頭による自己表現の練習も含まれています。さらに、英語を道具とした情報検索の方法を学ぶ機会も設け、内容理解のための活動をスパイラル式に織り交ぜているのが特徴です。どちらかというと英語が得意ではない学生（TOEICのスコアに換算すると350点前後）にも十分に楽しく参加してもらえるような工夫がなされています。

　本文は、ほぼ原文そのままのオーセンティックな英語で書かれており、上述の「読解前→読解→読解後」の流れで展開されるそれぞれの学習活動に取り組むことによって内容を重層的に理解でき、さらに発展学習にも取り組むことが可能な構成になっています。また、比較的英語が苦手な学生でも、美しい画像とともに、楽しみながら繰り返し学習することで効果的に成果が得られるように組み立ててあります。

　学生の皆さんが、本テキストを用いた最先端の科学情報や社会の出来事を読み解くという活動を通して、英語の基礎力を固め、英語で情報を収集したり自分の意見を表現したりできるようになることを願っています。

　最後になりましたが、本テキストの作成にあたり、丁寧に的確なご助言をくださったセンゲージ ラーニングの皆様に御礼を申し上げます。

編著者一同

TABLE OF CONTENTS

はしがき ……………………………………………………………………………… 3

本書の構成と効果的な使い方 …………………………………………………… 6

UNIT 1 Bare Bones By Brenna Maloney
私たちを支える骨の不思議 ……………………………………… 10
to ＋動詞の原形 [副詞用法]

UNIT 2 Mummy Mystery By Dr. Zahi Hawass
ツタンカーメンの死を探る ……………………………………… 16
be 動詞＋過去分詞（受動態）

UNIT 3 Swim with Seahorses By Lynn Brunelle
タツノオトシゴのユニークな生態 ……………………………… 22
It is ～ that ...

UNIT 4 Mission to Mars By Glen Phelan
火星有人飛行を目指して ………………………………………… 28
動名詞

UNIT 5 Feed the World By Gary Miller
食糧危機へのチャレンジ ………………………………………… 34
keep A from B

UNIT 6 Into the Rain Forest By Brenna Maloney
動物学者ジャングルをゆく ……………………………………… 40
help ＋人 [物]＋動詞の原形

UNIT 7 Turn Up the Heat By Alexandra Witze
氷の世界にそびえる活火山 ……………………………………… 46
～ enough to ＋動詞の原形

UNIT 8 Free Fall By Macon Morehouse
上空 39km から決死のダイブ！ ………………………………… 52
make it ～ to ＋動詞の原形

UNIT 9	**The Hidden Lives of Leaves** By Cynthia Overbeck Bix
	木の葉はみんな生きている ……………………………… *58*
	疑問詞＋S＋V（間接疑問）

UNIT 10	**Getting the Shot** By Marylou Tousignant
	海中撮影アドベンチャー ……………………………… *64*
	have ＋名詞＋過去分詞

UNIT 11	**Attack of the Germs** By Diane Wedner
	細菌を迎え撃つ体の秘密 ……………………………… *70*
	as ～ as S can

UNIT 12	**Just Like the Earth?** By Bethany Ehlmann with Beth Geiger
	宇宙からの物体を解明せよ！ ……………………………… *76*
	名詞＋分詞句／形容詞句／前置詞句

UNIT 13	**The Skin You're In** By Glen Phelan
	薄い皮膚の厚みある働きとは？ ……………………………… *82*
	some ... other(s) ～

UNIT 14	**Weirdest Wonders** By Glen Phelan
	息をのむ大地のダイナミズム ……………………………… *88*
	接続詞 as

UNIT 15	**Aquarius** By Joe Levit
	世界唯一の海中研究所へ潜入 *94*
	to ＋動詞の原形［形容詞用法］

Glossary ……………………………………………………………… *100*

本書の構成と効果的な使い方

本書は全15ユニットで構成されています。以下に、各ユニットの基本的な構成とアクティビティの特徴を説明します。

本文を読む前に

Check Your Vocabulary!

本文を理解する上で重要な語句、あるいは大学生として知っておくべき基本単語などを提示しています。自分の知っている語句（あるいは知らない語句）をチェックしながら、その Unit の内容を推測してみましょう。

本文の読解

Let's Read!

400語程度の本文を読みます。内容理解の助けになるような写真をなるべく多く入れています。最後に語注（NOTES）をつけてあります。

A 本文の内容理解を確認するための設問があります。選択肢などではなく、原則として自分の言葉で答えるようにしてあります。

B 本文の内容理解を確認するための True/False 問題。（※これがないユニットもあります）

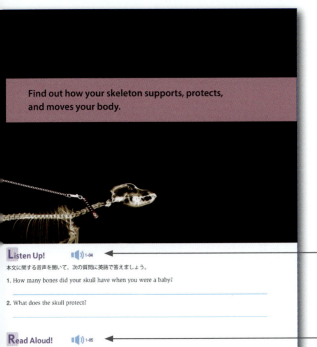

本文の読解後

Check the Form!

本文中にある一般的によく使われる語法や文法事項の確認と習得を目的としています。最初は意味を考えながらゆっくり発話する練習を行い、徐々にスピードを上げながら繰り返し練習するとよいでしょう。最終的には「日本語だけを見て英文がスラスラ言える」ことを目指して練習しましょう。

A 本文に出てきた重要な語法や文法事項を使った練習問題です。主に整序作文形式になっています。また、他のUnitの本文に出てくる文も問題として取り上げていることがあります。

B 本文に出てきた重要な語法や文法事項を使った口頭練習です。以下の2つのパターンを用意しています。ただ言えるのではなく、「すばやく言える」ことが大切です。

① **パターン・プラクティスによる言い替え演習：**
一人でもペアでも練習することができるようになっています。（pp. 14, 26, 38 など）

② **会話中の日本語を英語にしながら会話練習：**
英語は会話文の下に示してありますが、なるべくそれを見ないでスムーズに会話が言えるようになるまで繰り返し練習することが大切です。（pp. 21, 33, 57 など）

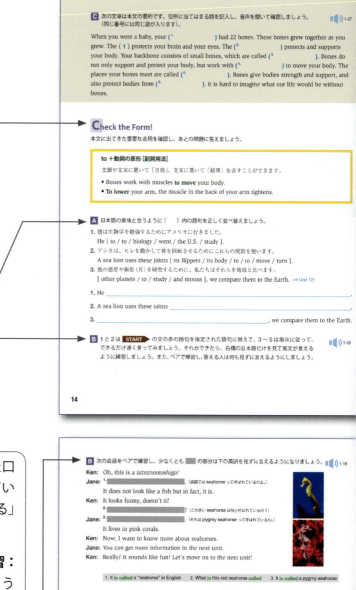

Now Listen to This!

ほぼ本文の内容に沿った会話やインタビューなどを聞き、その内容に関する質問に答える問題です。本文の復習も兼ねており、選択肢ではなく、自分で答えを書くようにしています。

It's Your Turn!

ユニットのトピックに関連した質問などに対して英語で答える練習です。Check the Form! で確認した語法や文法事項を活用しながら、自由に回答してみましょう。

Check It Out!

本文の内容理解をさらに深め広げるために、英語で書かれているインターネットの記事などにアクセスして、そこの情報を収集する活動です。その際、どのような語句を検索のキーワードにして情報を収集していくかということも重要になります。

音声ファイルの無料ダウンロード

http://cengage.jp/elt/JapaneseFourSkills/

🔊 1-00 のアイコンがある箇所の音声ファイルをダウンロードできます。

❶ 上記 URL にアクセスまたは QR コードをスマートフォンなどのリーダーでスキャン（→❹へ）
❷ 本書の表紙画像またはタイトル（Science Frontiers）をクリック
❸ 本書のページで 音声ファイル ボタンをクリック
❹ 希望の番号をクリックして音声ファイルをダウンロード

UNIT 1

Bare Bones

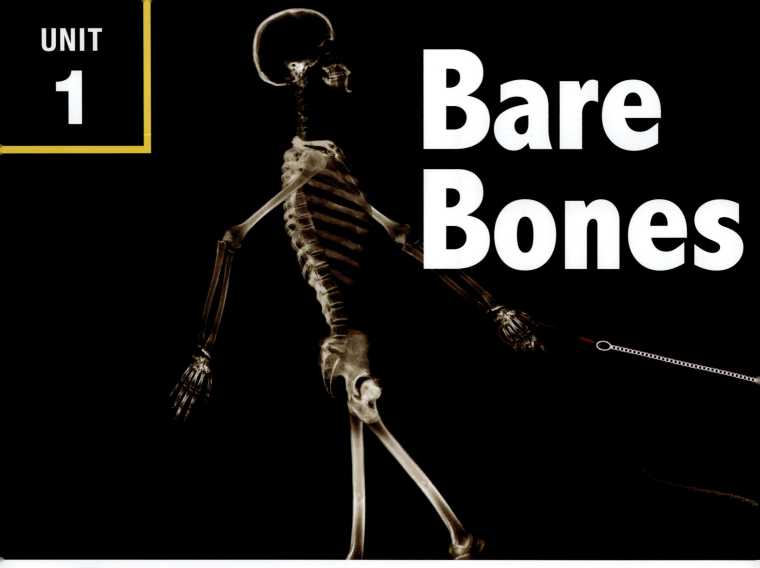

Check Your Vocabulary! 1-02~03

枠内から表の空所に当てはまる日本語や英語を選んで書き入れましょう。また、日本語には品詞も記入しましょう。
（N: 名詞　V: 動詞　Adj: 形容詞　Adv: 副詞）

skull	(N) 頭がい骨	lung	(N) 肺
protect	( )		(N) 臓器、器官
alike	( )		(N) 筋肉
thick	( )		(V) 曲げる、曲がる
thin	( )		(V) 引き締まる、きつくなる
backbone	( )		(Adv) 前へ
link	( )		(V) 下げる (Adj) 下方の
flat	( )		(N) 関節
form	( )		(Adv) 後ろへ

厚い、太い	頭がい骨	つなげる	bend	joint	muscle
薄い、細い	背骨	似ている	backward	lower	organ
形作る	平らな	保護する、守る	forward	lung	tighten

Find out how your skeleton supports, protects, and moves your body.

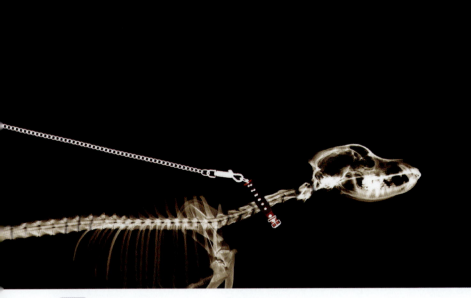

Listen Up! 1-04

本文に関する音声を聞いて、次の質問に英語で答えましょう。

1. How many bones did your skull have when you were a baby?

2. What does the skull protect?

Read Aloud! 1-05

背骨の役割や仕組みに注意して、次の文章を音読してみましょう。

> A backbone protects and supports your body. Your backbone is made up of lots of small bones. These bones are all linked together.

Let's Read! 🔊 1-06

次の文章を読んで、あとの問題に答えましょう。

Touch the back of your neck. Do you feel the bones in your neck? You have seven neck bones. Which do you think has the most neck bones—you, a mouse, or a giraffe? Surprise! The giraffe and mouse have seven, too. The giraffe's neck is longer because its bones are bigger.

Bone Basics

5 Bones are living things. They grow and change as you grow. As a baby, your skull had 22 bones. As you grow, these bones grow together. They form a shell around the brain. The skull protects your brain and your eyes.

    Not all skulls are alike. Take an elephant's skull, for example.
10 It is large and thick. It holds up the elephant's heavy trunk and tusks. A tarsier's skull is small and thin. It has large spaces to hold the animal's big eyes.

Lending Support

A backbone protects and supports your body. Your backbone is
15 made up of lots of small bones.

    These bones are all linked together. They're called vertebrae. That's why animals with backbones are called vertebrates.

    Together, vertebrae make a long tunnel. Your spinal cord runs through this tunnel. Your spinal cord is kept safe while it sends messages to and from your brain.

20   Ribs support and protect you, too. They are flat and curved. Ribs form a cage in your chest. Your heart, lungs, and some other organs nestle inside.

A tarsier

Bodies in Motion

Bones do more than support and protect your body. Bones work with muscles to move your body.

    Here's an example. Bend your arm. Your upper arm muscles go to work. The front muscle
25 tightens. It pulls the bones in your lower arm forward. Your elbow bends. To lower your arm, the muscle in the back of your arm tightens. Your arm pulls back.

    The place where bones meet is called a joint. Some joints work like a door hinge. They bend back and forth.

Bending and Turning

30 What looks like a flamingo's knee bends backward. Don't be fooled. That's its ankle. The bird's knee is hidden under feathers. Both joints work like hinges.

    Other joints help bones turn. Move your head left and right. Now move it up and down. That's your neck joint at work. An owl's neck joint lets it turn its head almost all the way around.

An eagle owl

35 **Putting Bones to Work**

Bones help you and other vertebrates get around. Bones give bodies strength and support. Bones also protect bodies from damage. Just imagine what your life would be like without bones.

> **NOTES**　trunk「(ゾウの) 鼻」　tusk「牙」　tarsier「メガネザル」　vertebra「脊椎、背骨」　vertebrate「脊椎動物」　spinal code「脊髄」　rib「肋骨」　nestle「具合よくおさまる」　hinge「蝶つがい」　ankle「足首、くるぶし」　owl「フクロウ」　get around「動き回る、歩き回る」

A 本文に関する次の質問に日本語で答えましょう。

Bone Basics

1. ゾウとメガネザルではそれぞれの頭がい骨にどのような特徴があるでしょうか。

　ゾウ:＿＿＿＿＿＿＿＿＿＿＿＿＿＿＿＿＿＿＿＿＿＿＿＿＿＿＿＿＿＿＿

　メガネザル:＿＿＿＿＿＿＿＿＿＿＿＿＿＿＿＿＿＿＿＿＿＿＿＿＿＿＿＿

Lending Support

2. vertebrae はどのような形状で何を保護しているでしょうか。

＿＿＿＿＿＿＿＿＿＿＿＿＿＿＿＿＿＿＿＿＿＿＿＿＿＿＿＿＿＿＿＿＿＿＿

Bodies in Motion

3. 腕を曲げるとき、筋肉と骨はどういう動きをするでしょうか。

＿＿＿＿＿＿＿＿＿＿＿＿＿＿＿＿＿＿＿＿＿＿＿＿＿＿＿＿＿＿＿＿＿＿＿

Bending and Turning

4. 関節は手や脚を曲げる以外に、どのような動きを助けますか。

＿＿＿＿＿＿＿＿＿＿＿＿＿＿＿＿＿＿＿＿＿＿＿＿＿＿＿＿＿＿＿＿＿＿＿

Putting Bones to Work

5. もし人間の体に骨がなかったら、どのような不都合が起こるでしょうか。

＿＿＿＿＿＿＿＿＿＿＿＿＿＿＿＿＿＿＿＿＿＿＿＿＿＿＿＿＿＿＿＿＿＿＿

B フラミンゴの骨の各部位について名称が正しければ T、間違っていれば F を丸で囲みましょう。F の場合は訂正しましょう。

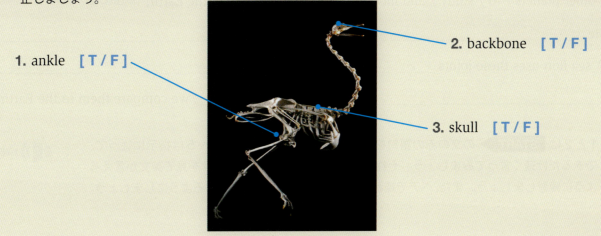

1. ankle　[T / F]
2. backbone　[T / F]
3. skull　[T / F]

C 次の文章は本文の要約です。空所に当てはまる語を記入し、音声を聞いて確認しましょう。
（同じ番号には同じ語が入ります）。 🔊 1-07

When you were a baby, your (¹.   ) had 22 bones. These bones grew together as you grew. The (1) protects your brain and your eyes. The (².   ) protects and supports your body. Your backbone consists of small bones, which are called (³.   ). Bones do not only support and protect your body, but work with (⁴.   ) to move your body. The places your bones meet are called (⁵.   ). Bones give bodies strength and support, and also protect bodies from (⁶.   ). It is hard to imagine what our life would be without bones.

Check the Form!

本文に出てきた重要な表現を確認し、あとの問題に答えましょう。

> **to ＋動詞の原形 [副詞用法]**
>
> 文頭や文末に置いて「目的」、文末に置いて「結果」を表すことができます。
>
> - Bones work with muscles **to move** your body.
> - **To lower** your arm, the muscle in the back of your arm tightens.

A 日本語の意味と合うように [   ] 内の語句を正しく並べ替えましょう。

1. 彼は生物学を勉強するためにアメリカに行きました。
   He [to / to / biology / went / the U.S. / study].
2. アシカは、ヒレを動かして体を回転させるためにこれらの関節を使います。
   A sea lion uses these joints [its flippers / its body / to / to / move / turn].
3. 他の惑星や衛星（月）を研究するために、私たちはそれらを地球と比べます。
   [other planets / to / study / and moons], we compare them to the Earth. (⇒ Unit 12)

1. He _____.

2. A sea lion uses these joints _____.

3. _____, we compare them to the Earth.

B 1と2は **START** の文の赤の語句を指定された語句に替えて、3〜5は指示に従って、できるだけ速く言ってみましょう。それができたら、右欄の日本語だけを見て英文が言えるように練習しましょう。また、ペアで練習し、答える人は何も見ずに言えるようにしましょう。

14

START ▶ I went to the United States **to study** music.（私は音楽を勉強しにアメリカへ行った。）

1. to study biology	→	I went to the United States to study biology.	私は生物学を勉強しにアメリカへ行った。
2. to see my friends	→	I went to the United States to see my friends.	私は友達に会いにアメリカへ行った。
3. 2の文をYes/No疑問文に	→	Did you go to the United States to see your friends?	君は友達に会いにアメリカへ行ったの？
4. 3の文をWhyを使った疑問文に	→	Why did you go to the United States?	なぜ君はアメリカへ行ったの？
5. 4の疑問文に対して答える文を	→	(I went) To see my friends.	友達に会いに（行ったんだ）。

Now Listen to This!

音声を聞いて、次の質問に日本語で答えましょう。

1. 人間の頭がい骨の骨は、どのように変わり、どんな役目を果たすでしょうか。

2. 人間の首の骨とキリンの首の骨は何が違うでしょうか。

3. 背骨は何を守っているでしょうか。

It's Your Turn!

次の質問に対する答えを完成させて、骨の機能を説明しましょう。また、ペアで会話してみましょう。

1. What is the main function of the skull bones?
   — It is _____.

2. What are two main purposes of the vertebrae?
   — They are _____.

3. Why do the bones work with the muscles of your body?
   — They work with the muscles _____.

Check It Out! 体を支え、脳や内臓を守る役割以外の骨の重要な役割をインターネットで調べてみましょう（検索のキーワードはbone marrow）。

UNIT 2

Mummy Mystery

Check Your Vocabulary! 1-10~11

枠内から表の空所に当てはまる日本語や英語を選んで書き入れましょう。また、日本語には品詞も記入しましょう。
(N: 名詞　V: 動詞　Adj: 形容詞　Adv: 副詞)

tomb	(N) 墓	strength	(N) 強さ、体力
bury	(　　)		(Adj) 活動的な、元気な
robber	(　　)		(N) ミイラ
steal	(　　)		(Adj) 骨折した
archaeologist	(　　)		(N) 画像
treasure	(　　)		(N) 病気
mystery	(　　)		(V) (病気)を患う
solve	(　　)		(Adj) 命にかかわるような
hunt	(　　)		(Adj) 弱い

埋める、埋葬する	考古学者	謎	active	disease	~~strength~~
解決する	強盗、盗賊	盗む	broken	image	suffer from
狩りをする	宝物	墓	deadly	mummy	weak

16

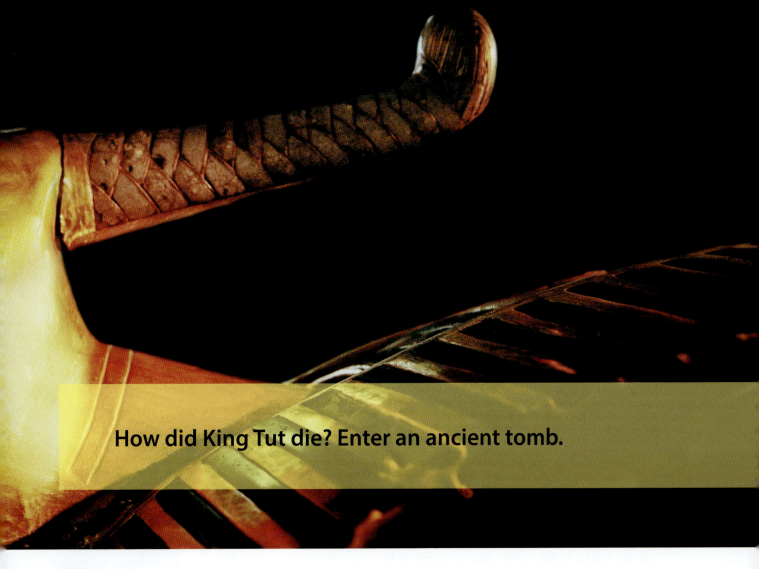

How did King Tut die? Enter an ancient tomb.

Listen Up! 1-12

本文に関する音声を聞いて、次の質問に英語で答えましょう。

1. What do people call Tutankhamen for short?

2. When was his tomb found?

Read Aloud! 1-13

次の文章は、ツタンカーメンのミイラのX線調査の説明です。発見された事実を思い浮かべながら、音読してみましょう。

> Scientists took x-rays of the mummy to find more answers. The x-rays show Tut had a broken leg. They also show a hole in his skull.

Let's Read! 1-14

次の文章を読んで、あとの問題に答えましょう。

Tomb Raiders

King Tut, whose full name is Tutankhamen, died about 3,000 years ago. He was buried in an area in Egypt with 62 other kings. So it's called the Valley of the Kings.

5   Robbers broke into many of the tombs. They stole all that they could carry. Yet they never found Tut's tomb. His tomb was hidden until 90 years ago. That's when archaeologists found it.

The Valley of the Kings

Crowning the Boy King

Treasures from the past are called artifacts. All of Tut's treasures were still inside his tomb. They tell an interesting story.

10   Tut grew up in a city called Amarna. His father was the king of Egypt. His name was Akhenaten. When his father died, Tut became king. He was about nine years old.

Because he was still a boy, Tut needed help to rule. Adults ruled for him. Just as Tut became old enough to rule on his own, he died. How he died has been a great mystery.

Royal Living

15   The artifacts in his tomb might help solve that mystery. Beads covered many of his shirts. He wore sparkling gold jewelry. He walked in fancy shoes.

He ate bread, cake, meat, and vegetables. For dessert, he liked honey, dates, and other fruits.

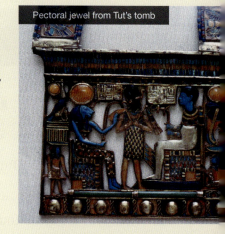

Pectoral jewel from Tut's tomb

20 ### The Warrior King

A golden fan in his tomb told me more. It shows Tut driving a chariot. It also shows him hunting and shooting arrows.

Both take lots of strength. Yet more than 100 canes were found in Tut's tomb. Why would such an active king need so many canes? What
25   do they tell us?

The Mummy's Secrets

Scientists took x-rays of the mummy to find more answers. The x-rays show Tut had a broken leg. They also show a hole in his skull. Did someone kill Tut? That was one theory.

Then I looked at Tut's mummy. My team used a CT scanner to take many pictures of Tut's
30   body. We used the pictures to make a 3-D image of him.

They told us that Tut was 19 when he died. He hadn't been murdered. The mummy makers had made the hole in his skull.

We also learned that Tut had a bone disease. His bones broke easily, so he needed help walking. That's why he had so many canes. Now that mystery was solved. Yet I still did not know
35   what had killed him.

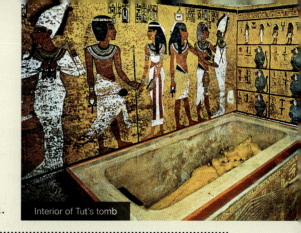

Testing Tut

I needed more information. So I tested Tut's bones. The test gave me the answer. Tut suffered from a deadly disease called malaria.

40　　I now knew how Tut died. His weak bones had made him sickly. An infection grew in his broken leg. The infection and the malaria killed him. I solved the mystery of King Tut's death.

Interior of Tut's tomb

NOTES the Valley of the Kings「王家の谷」 break into「…に侵入する、押し入る」 crown「…を王位につかせる」 artifact「人工遺物、埋蔵物」 chariot「戦闘や競技などに使われた古代の二輪馬車」 cane「杖」 x-ray「レントゲン写真」 CT scanner「コンピュータ断層撮影」 murder「殺す」

A 本文に関する次の質問に日本語で答えましょう。

Tomb Raiders
1. ツタンカーメンの墓は誰が発見したでしょうか。

Crowning the Boy King
2. ツタンカーメンが9歳で王位についたことは、どうしてわかったのでしょうか。

The Warrior King
3. 金色の扇からわかったことは何でしょうか。

The Mummy's Secrets
4. 結局、なぜ多くの杖が墓に埋葬されていたのでしょうか。

Testing Tut
5. 著者がツタンカーメンの骨を調べてわかったことは何でしょうか。

B 地図の示す内容と次の英文が合っていればT、間違っていればFを丸で囲みましょう。Fの場合は訂正しましょう。

1. Tut's tomb is in Sudan.　　[T / F]
2. There are two big rivers in Egypt.　　[T / F]

C 次の文章は本文の要約です。空所に当てはまる語を記入し、音声を聞いて確認しましょう。
（同じ番号には同じ語が入ります）

Tutankhamen died about 3,000 years ago. People call him King Tut for short. Although robbers stole many (1.   ) from tombs, they had never found Tut's tomb. When it was found about 90 years ago, the (1) from the past, which are called artifacts, told us an (2.   ) story about King Tut. A golden fan in his tomb shows Tut was driving a (3.   ), hunting and shooting arrows. However, more than 100 (4.   ) were also found in his tomb, making us wonder why such an active King needed them. The CT scanner pictures of King Tut told us that he had not been (5.   ). His skull did have a hole in it, but it was made by the mummy makers. Tut had a bone (6.   ), which is why he had so many (4). Finally, we found that he had suffered from malaria.

Check the Form!

本文に出てきた重要な表現を確認し、あとの問題に答えましょう。

---

be 動詞＋過去分詞（受動態）

「～される」という受け身の意味を表します。

- He **was buried** in an area in Egypt.
- His tomb **was hidden** until 90 years ago.
- Treasures from the past **are called** artifacts.

A 日本語の意味と合うように [　　] 内の語句を正しく並べ替えましょう。

1. あなたの背骨は多くの小さな骨で作られています。
   [is / lots of small bones / your backbone / made up of].
2. これらの骨はすべて連結されています。
   [are / all linked together / these bones].
3. それらは脊椎と呼ばれます。
   [are / they / vertebrae / called].

1. _____
2. _____
3. _____

B 次の会話をペアで練習し、少なくとも ▢ の部分は下の英訳を見ずに言えるようになりましょう。 🔊 1-16

Ken: Oh, this is a *tatsunootoshigo*!
Jane: 1. _____ .（英語では seahorse って呼ばれているのよ。）
It does not look like a fish but in fact, it is.
Ken: It looks funny, doesn't it?
2. _____ ?（この赤い seahorse は何と呼ばれているの？）
Jane: 3. _____ .（それは pygmy seahorse って呼ばれているわ。）
It lives in pink corals.
Ken: Now, I want to know more about seahorses.
Jane: You can get more information in the next unit.
Ken: Really? It sounds like fun! Let's move on to the next unit!

> 1. It **is called** a "seahorse" in English   2. What **is** this red seahorse **called**   3. It **is called** a pygmy seahorse

Now Listen to This! 🔊 1-17

音声を聞いて、次の質問に日本語で答えましょう。

1. King Tut の墓はどんな状態で発見されたでしょうか。
 _____

2. 100 個見つかったのは何でしょうか。
 _____

3. ミイラの骨を調べて何がわかったでしょうか。
 _____

It's Your Turn!

次の質問に対する答えを考えましょう。また、ペアで会話してみましょう。

1. When and by whom was Tutankhamen's tomb found?
 — _____ .

2. What was done with the mummy?
 — _____ .

3. Was Tutankhamen murdered? What was the cause of his death?
 — _____ .

Check It Out! 古代エジプトでは hieroglyphics（象形文字）が使用されていました。Egyptian hieroglyphic alphabet をキーワードにしてインターネットを検索し、自分の名前を象形文字で書いてみましょう。

UNIT 3

Swim with Seahorses

Check Your Vocabulary! 1-18~19

枠内から表の空所に当てはまる日本語や英語を選んで書き入れましょう。また、日本語には品詞も記入しましょう。
（N: 名詞　V: 動詞　Adj: 形容詞　Adv: 副詞）

dragon	(N) 竜		camouflage	(N) 偽装、擬態
barely	( )			(N) 海藻
seahorse	( )			(V) 変わる、…になる
survive	( )			(V) 消える
ocean	( )			(N) サンゴ
scale	( )			(Adj) ごく小さい
tip	( )			(Adv) 左右へ
tail	( )			(Adv) 上下に
stretch	( )			(V) 巻く

生き残る	海洋	タツノオトシゴ	~~camouflage~~	from side to side	turn
うろこ	かろうじて、なんとか	広がる	coral	seaweed	up and down
尾	先、先端	竜	disappear	tiny	wrap

22

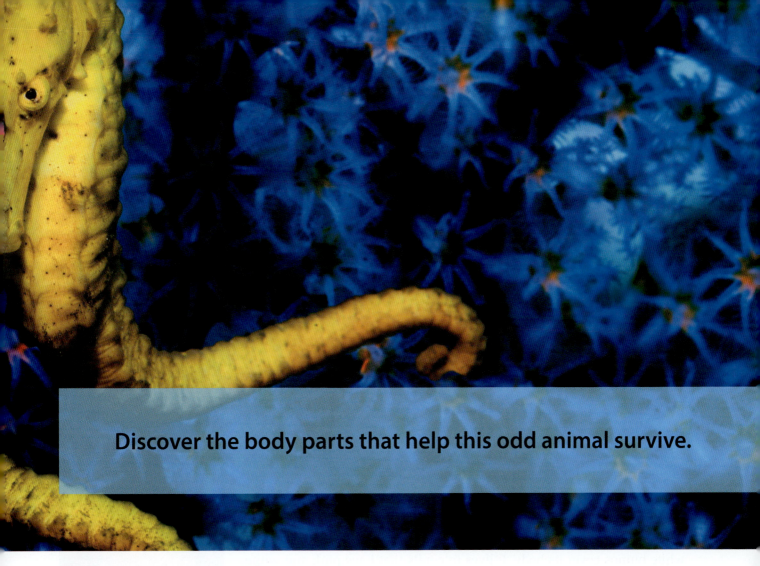

Discover the body parts that help this odd animal survive.

Listen Up! 1-20

本文に関する音声を聞いて、次の質問に英語で答えましょう。

1. What does a seahorse NOT have which most other fish have?

2. In what way can a seahorse protect itself?

Read Aloud! 1-21

タツノオトシゴが体の色を変化させる様子とその働きに注意して、次の文章を音読してみましょう。

> Let's say a pink seahorse swims in front of green seaweed. Its skin slowly starts to turn green. This change in color helps the seahorse blend in with the seaweed.

Let's Read! 1-22

次の文章を読んで、あとの問題に答えましょう。

It has the head of a horse, the body of a dragon, and the tail of a monkey. It has no teeth and no stomach. It lives in the sea, but this animal can barely swim. Meet the seahorse.

It may not look like a fish, but it is one. Each of its odd parts helps it survive in the ocean.

Rings of Plates

5 Seahorses swim in many oceans of the world. Some are as small as a bean. Others are as big as a banana.

Seahorses are vertebrates, like all fish. This means that all seahorses have backbones.

Most fish have tough scales that protect them. A seahorse doesn't. It has bony plates that protect its insides. The plates form rings that go from the top of the seahorse's neck to the tip of its
10 tail. A seahorse's thin skin stretches around the rings.

Blending In

A seahorse can protect itself another way, too. Its skin can change color. This is called camouflage.

Let's say a pink seahorse swims in front of green seaweed. Its skin
15 slowly starts to turn green. This change in color helps the seahorse blend in with the seaweed. It seems to disappear.

The pygmy seahorse uses another kind of camouflage. Pink and white bumps cover its body. It lives in corals that have pink and white bumps. The pygmy seahorse is hard to see when it swims into these
20 corals. So they're great places for this seahorse to hide from predators.

A pygmy seahorse

Getting Around

It's good that seahorses can hide because they aren't fast swimmers. They don't swim the same way other fish do. Most fish have strong tail fins. They wiggle their tail fins to zip through the water.

25 The seahorse doesn't have a tail fin. It has a tiny fin on its back. It flutters this fin to swim forward. It has two small fins on its head, too. It uses them to move from side to side.

Another part of a seahorse's body helps it to move up and down. This part is called a swim bladder. It's like a balloon inside the seahorse's body. To float, the seahorse fills the bladder with air. To sink, the seahorse lets out some of the air.

30 ### Touching with Tails

The seahorse doesn't use its tail for swimming. Yet it does use its tail for something else.

The seahorse wraps its tail around plants to stay in place. Now, strong waves can't sweep it away.

35 **Seahorse Survival**
The life of a seahorse is full of danger. It struggles to stay alive. Yet no other animal is built like a seahorse. Its odd mix of body parts helps it to survive.

> **NOTES** odd「変わった、奇妙な」 vertebrate「脊椎動物」 blend in (with)「…に溶け込む」 pygmy seahorse「ピグミーシーホース」 bump「突起」 predator「捕食者（天敵など）」 wiggle「…をくねくね動かす」 zip「勢いよく進む」 flutter「…をパタパタさせる」 swim bladder「(魚の) 浮き袋」

A 本文に関する次の質問に答えましょう。特に指示のない場合は日本語で答えましょう。

1. タツノオトシゴはどのような特徴を持つ生物でしょうか。
___

Rings of Plates
2. 次のうちタツノオトシゴが持っているものを丸で囲みましょう。

   薄い皮膚　　うろこ　　背骨　　尾　　環状の骨板

Blending In
3. ピグミーシーホースの擬態は、具体的に何が何のように見えるのでしょうか。
___

Getting Around
4. タツノオトシゴはどのようにして左右に、また上下に移動するのでしょうか。

   左右: ___

   上下: ___

Seahorse Survival
5. 本文に full of danger とありますが、例えばどのような危険なのでしょうか。
___

B 写真についての説明が正しければT、間違っていればFを丸で囲みましょう。Fの場合は訂正しましょう。

1. It does not have scales.　　[T / F]

2. It has the head of a horse.　[T / F]

long neck / strong snout / powerful back fin / gripping tail

C 次の文章は本文の要約です。空所に当てはまる語を記入し、音声を聞いて確認しましょう。 1-23

Seahorses have no teeth and no stomach. Like all fish, seahorses are vertebrates, which means that all seahorses have (1.   ). Most fish have tough (2.   ) to protect them, but a seahorse has bony plates to protect its insides. A seahorse can also protect itself by changing its skin color, which is called (3.   ). It's good for seahorses that they can (4.   ) because they are not fast swimmers. Most fish (5.   ) their tail fins to move quickly through water. The seahorses swim forward by (6.   ) tiny fins on their backs, and they move up and down by using a swim bladder. The seahorse's strange and unique body parts help it to stay alive in the sea.

Check the Form!

本文に出てきた重要な表現を確認し、あとの問題に答えましょう。

> **It is ~ that ...** 「…なのは~だ」
>
> that ... は、仮主語 it の内容を表します。
>
> • **It's** good **that** seahorses can hide.

A 意味を考えながら、[　]内の語句を正しく並べ替えましょう。

1. [that / it / certain / succeed / will / is / he] in the new business.
2. [it / he / was not / the difficult exam / surprising / that / passed].
3. [was / it / had / the nuclear power plant / that / a serious accident / shocking].

1. _____ in the new business.
2. _____.
3. _____.

B START ▶ の文の赤と青の語句を 1～4 の指定された語句に替えて、できるだけ速く言ってみましょう。それができたら、右欄の日本語だけを見て英文が言えるように練習しましょう。また、ペアで練習し、答える人は何も見ずに言えるようにしましょう。 1-24

26

START　It was **lucky** that I got the concert ticket. (私がそのコンサートチケットを手に入れたのは幸運だった。)

1. unlucky	I missed the train	→	It was unlucky that I missed the train.	私が列車に乗り遅れたのは不運だった。
2. cruel	many people were killed in the war	→	It was cruel that many people were killed in the war.	多くの人がその戦争で亡くなったのは残酷だった。
3. surprising	he won over the famous player	→	It was surprising that he won over the famous player.	彼がその有名な選手に勝ったのは驚きだった。
4. understandable	you didn't accept his offer	→	It was understandable that you didn't accept his offer.	君が彼の申し出を受けなかったのは理解できた。

Now Listen to This!

音声を聞いて、次の質問に日本語で答えましょう。

1. 話題になっている生き物は、なぜタツノオトシゴと日本語で呼ばれるのでしょうか。
   _____

2. 一般的な魚とどんな共通点を持っているでしょうか。
   _____

3. 一般的な魚とどんな異なる点を持っているでしょうか。
   _____

It's Your Turn!

空所に適当な語句を入れて、会話を完成させましょう。また、ペアで会話してみましょう。

1. Our teacher is really nice. I think it is _____ that he _____
   _____.
   — Yes, in addition, he is good at teaching, so every student likes him.

2. It was so _____ that the photographer _____
   _____.
   — Yes, but his photos of marine creatures are really beautiful. I think that is the reason the TV show featured him.

3. It is _____ that so many people _____.
   — Exactly. Wars kill many people, so we must find a way to avoid any kind of war.

Check It Out! タツノオトシゴの生物分類の属名は *Hippocampus* といいます。この語源の意味を調べてみましょう。また、*Legionella* の語源・名前の由来を探してみましょう。

UNIT 4
Mission to Mars

Check Your Vocabulary! 1-26~27

枠内から表の空所に当てはまる日本語や英語を選んで書き入れましょう。また、日本語には品詞も記入しましょう。
（N: 名詞　V: 動詞　Adj: 形容詞　Adv: 副詞）

Mars	(N) 火星		gravity	(N) 重力
farther	( )			(V) 口論する
fuel	( )			(Adj) 悪い、誤った
crew	( )			(N) 解決法
radiation	( )			(V) 対処する
spaceship	( )			(Adj) 片道の
block	( )			(N) 居留地
invent	( )			(N) 酸素
astronaut	( )			(V) 呼吸する

宇宙船	遮る	発明する、創り出す	argue	~~gravity~~	oxygen
宇宙飛行士	燃料	放射線	breathe	handle	solution
~~火星~~	乗組員	もっと遠くに	colony	one-way	wrong

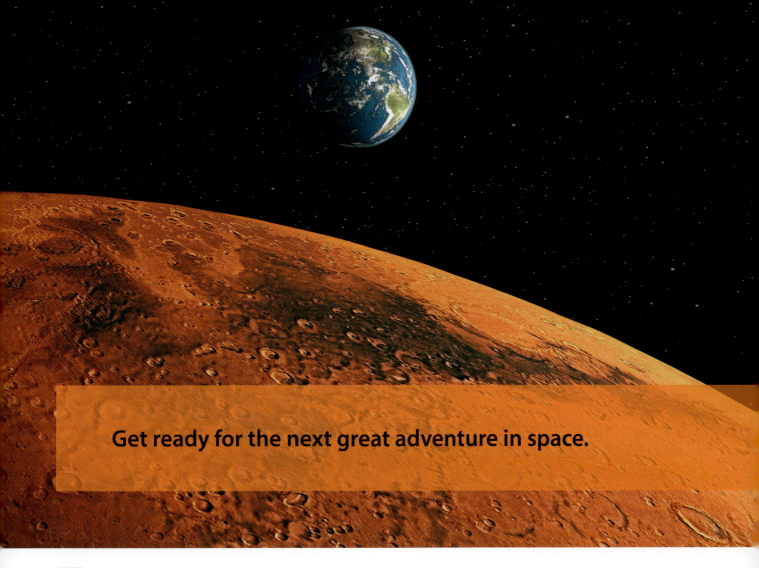

Get ready for the next great adventure in space.

Listen Up!

本文に関する音声を聞いて、次の質問に英語で答えましょう。

1. How long would it take to get to Mars?

2. What can cause cancer and even kill people in space?

Read Aloud!

宇宙飛行士が宇宙で注意すべき点などについて理解しながら、次の文章を音読してみましょう。

> It's important that the crew members get along, too. They'll be cooped up together for a long time. They might become restless. They may argue.

Let's Read! 1-30

次の文章を読んで、あとの問題に答えましょう。

Around the world, scientists are working together to put humans on Mars. It won't be easy.

Going to Mars isn't a short trip. At its closest, Mars is 150 times farther away from us than our moon is. Using the fuel in today's rockets, it would take about six months to get there. That's a long trip.

An Atlas V rocket carrying NASA's Mars rover dubbed *Curiosity*

A Safe Crew

There are many dangers in space. One danger is radiation. It is a form of energy that can harm people. It can cause cancer and even kill people.

Luckily, spaceships do block some radiation. Spacesuits block more of it, but not all. Something stronger needs to be invented. Engineers are working on this problem now.

A Healthy Crew

There are other problems astronauts face, too. Long trips in space can weaken bones. On the Earth, bones stay healthy when muscles pull on them. The muscles fight against gravity. There is no gravity in space. So bones grow weak.

Astronauts are already testing a new exercise machine. It makes the astronauts feel like they are pushing against gravity.

Scientists are also studying a new medicine. It will keep bones from becoming weak.

Picking the Right Crew

It's important that the crew members get along, too. They'll be cooped up together for a long time. They might become restless. They may argue.

Yet all of the astronauts need to get along. If something goes wrong, they will have to find a solution. It would take too long to get help from the Earth. The crew needs to handle emergencies together.

One-Way Mission?

After the rockets and the crew are ready to go, it's time for the next step. Some scientists think the next step is to go to Mars. They think crews should make a short visit to Mars, then go back to the Earth. Others think a Mars trip should be one-way. They believe a Mars colony could be set up within 10 years.

Surviving on Mars

To live on Mars, people will need water, air, and food. Luckily, Mars has some resources. It has ice. The ice could be taken from the ground for drinking and washing. Oxygen in the water could make air to breathe.

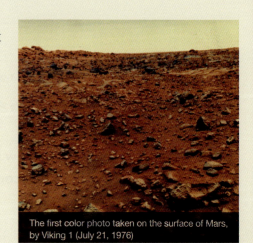

The first color photo taken on the surface of Mars, by Viking 1 (July 21, 1976)

35 **Decisions, Decisions**
Learning more about Mars and space travel is very important.
It will help astronauts and engineers make decisions.
   By working together, humans may one day reach Mars.
Then the people of the Earth can call the Red Planet home, too.

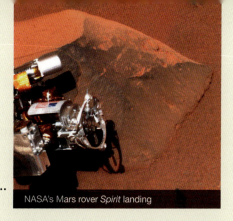
NASA's Mars rover *Spirit* landing

NOTES get along 「うまくいく、仲良くする」 be cooped up 「閉じこもる」
restless 「不安な、落ち着かない」

A 本文に関する次の質問に日本語で答えましょう。

A Safe Crew
1. 宇宙船と宇宙服では、どちらのほうがより放射線を防ぐことができるでしょうか。

A Healthy Crew
2. 宇宙空間で乗組員たちの骨が弱くならないように、どんな方法が準備されているでしょうか。

Picking the Right Crew
3. なぜ乗組員たちの人間関係（仲良くするよう）に気を配らなければならないのでしょうか。

One-Way Mission?
4. 一部の科学者たちは、短期滞在の他に火星で何ができると考えているでしょうか。

Surviving on Mars
5. 4. を考える際、火星のどういうことが前提となっているでしょうか。

B 右の火星に関する情報の説明として英文が正しければT、間違っていればFを丸で囲みましょう。Fの場合は訂正しましょう。

1. Mars is bigger than the Earth.　　[T / F]
2. A year on Mars is almost twice as long as an Earth year.　[T / F]

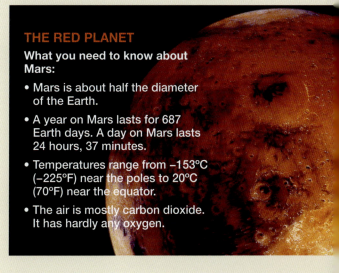

THE RED PLANET
What you need to know about Mars:
- Mars is about half the diameter of the Earth.
- A year on Mars lasts for 687 Earth days. A day on Mars lasts 24 hours, 37 minutes.
- Temperatures range from −153°C (−225°F) near the poles to 20°C (70°F) near the equator.
- The air is mostly carbon dioxide. It has hardly any oxygen.

UNIT 4 ■ Mission to Mars　31

C 次の文章は本文の要約です。空所に当てはまる語を記入し、音声を聞いて確認しましょう。　1-31

It takes a long time to get to Mars. It would take about six months to get there. During the long trip, there are many dangers in space, such as (1.   ), which can cause cancer and even kill people. There are other problems (2.   ) face in the trip, too. Their bones become weak as there is no (3.   ) in space. Some scientists think that a Mars trip should be one-way rather than coming back to the Earth after visiting Mars. They believe a Mars (4.   ) can be made within 10 years. Mars has some (5.   ) to live on, like ice. The ice could be taken out from the ground, and (6.   ) in the water could produce air to breathe.

Check the Form!

本文に出てきた重要な表現を確認し、あとの問題に答えましょう。

> **動名詞（-ing）**
>
> 「～すること」という意味を表し、文中で名詞と同じ場所に用いられます。
>
> - **Going** to Mars isn't a short trip.
> - The ice could be taken from the ground for **drinking** and **washing**.
> - **Learning** more about Mars and space travel is very important.
> - By **working** together, humans may one day reach Mars.

A 意味を考えながら、[　　]内の語句を正しく並べ替えましょう。

1. [could / be / swimming / dangerous / in the middle of a lot of jellyfish]. (⇒ Unit 10)
2. Wash your hands [after / and before / playing / eating].
3. By [of / care / your body / taking], you'll feel better. (⇒ Unit 11)

1. _____.

2. Wash your hands _____.

3. By _____, you'll feel better.

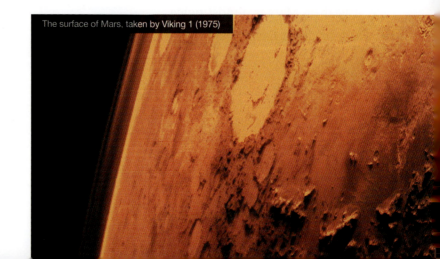

The surface of Mars, taken by Viking 1 (1975)

B 次の会話をペアで練習し、少なくとも ▢ の部分は下の英訳を見ずに言えるようになりましょう。 🔊 1-32

John: 1. _____. （火星に行くのは短い旅じゃないんだ。）

Mary: Exactly. It would take about six months to get there if we use today's rockets. 2. _____? （新しいロケットを開発したらどうかしら？）

John: That's a good point. NASA is building a new rocket now.

Mary: Oh, that's great!

John: There is another problem, though.

Mary: What do you mean?

John: 3. _____. （仲良くすることが乗組員にとっては大切なんだ。）

Mary: I see. They will be cooped up together for a long time, so they might argue.

John: That's right. Yet they must work together to handle emergencies.

1. **Going** to Mars isn't a short trip   2. How about **inventing** a new rocket   3. **Getting** along is important for the crew members

Now Listen to This!   🔊 1-33

音声を聞いて、次の質問に日本語で答えましょう。

1. 人類が火星に居留地を設立できるかもしれないのは何年後ですか。

   _____

2. なぜ放射線を防がなければならないのですか。

   _____

3. さまざまな問題が解決されたら、あなたは火星に行ってみたいですか。

   _____

It's Your Turn!

次の質問に対する自分の答えを完成させましょう。また、ペアで会話してみましょう。

1. Would you like to try living on Mars?

   — [Yes / No], _____.

2. Do you like traveling? Where do you like to go?

   — [Yes / No], _____.

3. Have you finished packing for your trip next week?

   — [Yes / No], _____.

Check It Out! 一般の人々のための宇宙旅行を扱う会社があります。space travel をキーワードに会社の名前をインターネットで検索して、宇宙旅行の内容を調べてみましょう。

UNIT 5

Discover new ways farmers hope to

Feed the World

Check Your Vocabulary! 🔊 1-34~35

枠内から表の空所に当てはまる日本語や英語を選んで書き入れましょう。また、日本語には品詞も記入しましょう。
（N: 名詞　V: 動詞　Adj: 形容詞　Adv: 副詞）

population	(N) 人口	terrace		(N) 段々畑
feed	( )			(Adj) 垂直の
struggle	( )			(Adj) 安全な
reshape	( )			(N) 害虫
crop	( )			(N) 天気
ancient	( )			(N) 量
nutrient	( )			(Adj) 室内の
turn	( )			(V) 積み重ねる
hungry	( )			(N) 農地

飢えた	苦労する	人口	amount	pest	~~terrace~~
栄養分	古代の	食べ物を与える	farmland	safe	vertical
回転する	作物	作り変える	indoor	stack	weather

Listen Up! 🔊 1-36

本文に関する音声を聞いて、次の質問に英語で答えましょう。

1. Who is looking for new ways of farming?

2. What do people call the Incas' way of farming?

Read Aloud! 🔊 1-37

次の文章は、室内農法の仕組みについての説明です。光や水、養分の供給の仕方に注意して、音読してみましょう。

> Trays of plants are stacked inside a frame like a giant Ferris wheel. The frame slowly turns. Each plant gets equal amounts of light, water, and nutrients.

Let's Read! 🔊 1-38

次の文章を読んで、あとの問題に答えましょう。

The Earth's population is growing fast. Everyone needs to eat, but feeding everyone is a big challenge. Farmers and scientists are looking for new ways to grow food.

Looking for Answers

Not having enough food is not a new problem. Even the earliest farmers struggled with using the Earth's natural resources. Sometimes, the land wasn't good for farming. It was too dry, too wet, or too rugged.

To solve the problem, farmers changed the land. They reshaped it. They cut down trees or built dams. They made it easier to grow crops.

Taking the Right Steps

The Incas were farmers who changed their land. They were an ancient people in South America. There were more than 12 million Incas to feed.

They lived in the mountains where food was hard to grow. Water flowed down the slopes and washed away the soil. Water carried away the nutrients in the soil, too.

So the Incas carved huge steps into the side of the mountains. They built stone walls around each step. They made flat land to plant their crops.

These terraces looked like giant steps. Rainwater flowed into each step. The soil soaked up the water. The walls kept the soil from washing away. To this day, many people still farm this way. It's called terrace farming.

Farming the Sky

Land is hard to find in Singapore. More than five million people live there. This city in Asia needs to produce a lot of food to feed all the people. There isn't enough land to plant crops, though.

Some farmers think they have the answer. They want to grow food inside tall buildings. It's called vertical farming.

Inside, the plants stay safe from pests and bad weather. Farmers control the amount of nutrients, light, and water for each plant.

Here's how it works at one indoor farm. Trays of plants are stacked inside a frame like a giant Ferris wheel. The frame slowly turns. Each plant gets equal amounts of light, water, and nutrients.

This new technology is still being tested. If it works, it could be a solution for places that don't have a lot of farmland.

Feeding the World

The Earth's population is growing. More and more people need to be fed. This could become a big problem.

Don't worry. Farmers and scientists are hard at work. They're finding new ways to help feed our hungry planet.

NOTES natural resources「天然資源」 carve「切り開く」 soak up「吸収する」 Ferris wheel「観覧車」

A 本文に関する次の質問に日本語で答えましょう。

Looking for Answers

1. 昔の農業従事者（農民）たちは、作物を育てやすくするためにどのようなことをしたでしょうか。

___

Taking the Right Steps

2. 古代インカの人々が山で作物を育てるのに、困ったことは何だったでしょうか。

___

3. 2の「困ったこと」をどのように解決したでしょうか。

___

Farming the Sky

4. シンガポールの人々が作物を育てようとした際に問題だったことは何でしょうか。

___

5. 解決策として行われた方法が「観覧車みたい」というのはどのようなことでしょうか。

___

B それぞれの写真に合う地名とそこで行われる農法名を丸で囲みましょう。

1. 地名： Peru / Singapore
   農法名：vertical farming / terrace farming

2. 地名： Peru / Singapore
   農法名：vertical farming / terrace farming

UNIT 5　Feed the World　**37**

C 次の文章は本文の要約です。空所に当てはまる語を記入し、音声を聞いて確認しましょう。　1-39

Farmers and scientists are looking for new ways to grow food because the Earth's population is growing fast. Not having enough food has been a problem for a long time. The earliest farmers also (1.　　　　) with using the Earth's natural resources because the land was sometimes too dry, wet or (2.　　　　). The Incas' way of farming is called (3.　　　　) farming. They changed their land for farming by (4.　　　　) huge steps into the side of the mountains. They built (5.　　　　) walls around each step and made flat land for farming. On the other hand, some farmers want to grow food inside tall buildings when there is not enough land to plant crops. It is called (6.　　　　) farming.

Check the Form!

本文に出てきた重要な表現を確認し、あとの問題に答えましょう。

> **keep A from B**「A を B から遠ざけておく、A を B から守る」
>
> B のところには名詞や動名詞が入ります。
>
> • The walls **kept** *the soil* **from** *washing away*.

A 意味を考えながら、[　]内の語句を正しく並べ替えましょう。

1. Cold weather [blooming / kept / from / the cherry blossoms].
2. We [the bad news / from / keep / should] her.
3. Vertical farming [from / keeps / damage due to pests and bad weather / crops].

1. Cold weather _____.
2. We _____ her.
3. Vertical farming _____.

B 1〜3は START の文の赤と青の語句を指定された語句に替えて、4と5は指示に従って、できるだけ速く言ってみましょう。それができたら、右欄の日本語だけを見て英文が言えるように練習しましょう。また、ペアで練習し、答える人は何も見ずに言えるようにしましょう。　1-40

Hydroponic vegetable plantation system

START We should **keep** children **from** the influenza virus.
（子供をインフルエンザウイルスから遠ざけておかなければならない。）

1. these papers	getting wet	→ We should keep these papers from getting wet.	これらの書類を濡れないように保たなければならない。
2. our dog	harmful insects	→ We should keep our dog from harmful insects.	私たちの犬を害虫から守らなければならない。
3. this news	Jane	→ We should keep this news from Jane.	この知らせをジェーンに知らせないでおくべきだ。
4. 3の文をYes/No疑問文に		→ Should we keep this news from Jane?	この知らせをジェーンに知らせないでおくべきかな？
5. 4の疑問文にNoで答える		→ No, we don't need to.	いや、その必要はないよ。

Now Listen to This! 1-41

音声を聞いて、次の質問に日本語で答えましょう。

1. 土地が乾燥して農地に適していないときはどうしましたか。

2. 平らな土地がないときはどうしましたか。

3. 垂直農法はどこで行いましたか。

It's Your Turn!

次の質問に対する答えを考えて完成させましょう。また、ペアで会話してみましょう。

1. How can farmers keep the water from washing away the soil?
   — They can _____.

2. How can farmers keep plants safe from pests?
   — They can _____.

3. How can we keep people from starving?
   — We can _____.

Check It Out! 日本や世界におけるvertical farmingについてインターネットで検索し、情報を集めてみましょう。どのような作物がどのように育てられているでしょうか。

UNIT 6

Into the Rain Forest

Check Your Vocabulary! 1-42~43

枠内から表の空所に当てはまる日本語や英語を選んで書き入れましょう。また、日本語には品詞も記入しましょう。
(N: 名詞　V: 動詞　Adj: 形容詞　Adv: 副詞)

wild	(Adj) 野生の	long-sleeved	(Adj) 長袖の
zoologist	( )		(Adj) 冷静な
once	( )		(N) 訪問者
frog	( )		(N) ゴキブリ
carefully	( )		(N) 小屋
bug spray	( )		(N) 道具
costume	( )		(Adj) 毒性の、有毒な
meal	( )		(N) 毒
challenge	( )		(N) 生き物

衣装	食事	難題	calm	gear	poison
カエル	注意深く、入念に	虫除けスプレー	cockroach	hut	toxic
かつて、昔	動物学者	野生の	creature	long-sleeved	visitor

Join explorer Lucy Cooke as she looks for the world's oddest frogs.

Listen Up! 1-44

本文に関する音声を聞いて、次の質問に英語で答えましょう。

1. What is Lucy Cooke's job? What does she study?

2. What do you need when you are exploring?

Read Aloud! 1-45

自然の中を探検する際に適した服装に注意して、次の文章を音読してみましょう。

> Don't worry about looking good. Baggy pants, a long-sleeved shirt, and a T-shirt will do. That's the explorer's uniform.

Let's Read! 1-46

次の文章を読んで、あとの問題に答えましょう。

Lucy Cooke studies wild animals in wild places. She's a zoologist.
    Cooke's love of animals started when she was a kid. Once, she saw a TV show about frogs. One of the frogs was a waxy monkey frog. She loved the frog. So Cooke began to study frogs.

A waxy monkey frog

5   Cooke still studies frogs and other amphibians. To find them, she goes into rain forests where they live. Whenever she travels, there are a few tips she lives by. Cooke likes to share these tips with other explorers.

Pack Carefully

Think about what you carry in your school backpack. Cooke carries boots, bug spray, and a
10 headlamp. She also carries a frog mask and cape. She uses this costume to teach people about frogs.

Bring What You Need

You would need boots to keep your feet dry. Snakes and leeches live in the rain forest. You don't want to get bitten by them. Boots will protect your feet and ankles from them.
15   Bug spray is also good to carry. It'll keep biting bugs away. Make sure the spray is safe for other wildlife, though. This is important.
    A headlamp helps you see into the dark forest. It can also help you spot frogs hiding under plants.

Forget Fashion

20 Don't worry about looking good. Baggy pants, a long-sleeved shirt, and a T-shirt will do. That's the explorer's uniform.
    Long sleeves and pants will protect your arms and legs.

Expect Simple Meals

Meal time in the rain forest can be a challenge. First, most of the food you need has to be carried.
25 So you can't bring too much. Second, fresh foods don't stay fresh for long. So what you bring can't spoil. Third, to cook, you must build a fire.

Keep You Cool

Explorers need to be ready for anything. Whatever happens, an explorer must keep calm.

Remember, You're the Guest

30 In the rain forest, humans are the visitors. Cooke learned this on one trip. Cockroaches had moved into her hut.
    The bugs were in her sleeping bag, in her gear, and in her clothes. They crawled over her toothbrush, too! Cooke washed the toothbrush and put it away. After all, she was the visitor. The toothbrush was in the cockroaches' way.

Listen to Your Teammates

Recently, Cooke was looking for a toxic frog. It has enough poison on its skin to kill 15 people.

"For 25 years, I had wanted to see this creature," Cooke says. "When I finally did, I burst into tears." She moved to wipe away the tears. "STOP!" her team yelled. She stopped. Her glove was coated in the frog's poison. One touch and she could have died.

An explorer's job is not easy.

A golden poison frog

NOTES amphibian「両生類」 rain forest「熱帯雨林」 after all「結局」

A 本文に関する次の質問に答えましょう。特に指示のない場合は日本語で答えましょう。

Pack Carefully
1. カエルのマスクとケープは何のために持って行くのでしょうか。

Bring What You Need
2. 虫除けスプレーを使う際に気を付けることは何でしょうか。

Expect Simple Meals
3. 食事の持ち物として適切でないものを丸で囲みましょう。

　　fresh vegetables　　canned foods　　lighter　　raw egg　　rice

Remember, You're the Guest
4. ゴキブリはなぜ歯ブラシの上を這って行ったのでしょうか。

Listen to Your Teammates
5. チームメートはなぜ「STOP!」と叫んだのでしょうか。

B この写真で、チームメートが探検に出かけるために守っている服装を英語で2つ挙げましょう。

1. _____
2. _____

C 次の文章は本文の要約です。空所に当てはまる語を記入し、音声を聞いて確認しましょう。　1-47

Lucy Cooke is a (1.　　　　　　). She studies frogs and other amphibians. There are some
(2.　　　　　　) for traveling with other explorers. If you are exploring you would need
(3.　　　　　　) to keep your feet dry, which prevents you from being (4.　　　　　　) by
snakes and leeches. As for fashion, long sleeves and pants will (5.　　　　　　) your arms and
legs as plants can scratch and bugs can bite. In the rain forest, humans are the (6.　　　　　　).
Cooke learned this through her experiences with bugs. An explorer's job is not easy.

Check the Form!

本文に出てきた重要な表現を確認し、あとの問題に答えましょう。

> **help ＋人[物]＋動詞の原形**「人[物]が…するのを助ける／…するのに役立つ」
>
> 「動詞の原形」の前に to が付くこともあります。
>
> - A headlamp **helps you see** into the dark forest.
> - It can also **help you spot** frogs hiding under plants.

A 意味を考えながら、[　　]内の語句を正しく並べ替えましょう。

1. Joints [turn / help / bones]. (⇒ Unit 1)
2. You can [do / help / its work / your immune system]. (⇒ Unit 11)
3. Another part of a seahorse's body [it / move up and down / to / helps]. (⇒ Unit 3)

1. Joints _____.

2. You can _____.

3. Another part of a seahorse's body _____.

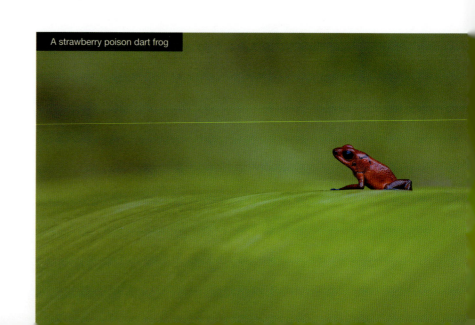

A strawberry poison dart frog

B START の文の赤の語句を1〜4の指定された語句に替えて、できるだけ速く言ってみましょう。それができたら、右欄の日本語だけを見て英文が言えるように練習しましょう。
また、ペアで練習し、答える人は何も見ずに言えるようにしましょう。

START Will you **help me clean** this room?（この部屋を掃除するのを手伝ってくれない？）

1. do my homework	➡ Will you help me do my homework?	宿題するのを手伝ってくれない？
2. cook dinner	➡ Will you help me cook dinner?	夕食を作るのを手伝ってくれない？
3. carry this heavy bag	➡ Will you help me carry this heavy bag?	この重いかばんを運ぶのを手伝ってくれない？
4. look for a toxic frog	➡ Will you help me look for a toxic frog?	毒ガエルを探すのを手伝ってくれない？

Now Listen to This!

音声を聞いて、次の質問に日本語で答えましょう。

1. どんな内容の話でしょうか。
   _____

2. なぜ長袖シャツと長ズボンを着用する必要があるのでしょうか。
   _____

3. "you are the guest" とは、どういうことを言いたいのでしょうか。
   _____

It's Your Turn!

次の質問に対する答えを考えましょう。また、ペアで会話してみましょう。

1. Why should you wear boots?
   — _____.

2. Why do you need a headlamp?
   — _____.

3. Why should you always try to keep calm?
   — _____.

Check It Out! rain forest はどのように定義されるでしょうか。また、rain forest は「世界最大の薬局」と呼ばれていますが、その理由は何でしょうか。

UNIT 6　Into the Rain Forest

UNIT 7

Turn Up the Heat

Check Your Vocabulary! 1-50~51

枠内から表の空所に当てはまる日本語や英語を選んで書き入れましょう。また、日本語には品詞も記入しましょう。
(N: 名詞　V: 動詞　Adj: 形容詞　Adv: 副詞)

steam	(N)水蒸気	*freeze*		(V)凍る
Antarctica	( )			(Adj)氷の（ような）
volcano	( )			(N)中心部、核
blow	( )			(N)表面
lava	( )			(V)噴出する
melt	( )			(V)落ちる
stink	( )			(N)圧力
cave	( )			(Adv)ほぼ、ほとんど
crystal	( )			(N)噴火

悪臭を放つ	水蒸気	南極大陸	core	freeze	pressure
火山	洞窟、洞穴	吹く、吐く	eruption	icy	spurt
結晶	融ける	溶岩	fall	nearly	surface

Visit some of the oddest volcanoes on the Earth.

Listen Up! 🔊 1-52

本文に関する音声を聞いて、次の質問に英語で答えましょう。

1. Where is Mt. Erebus?

2. What makes Mt. Erebus an odd volcano?

Read Aloud! 🔊 1-53

次の文章は、火山の噴火口内の様子を説明しています。匂いや状況を想像しながら、音読してみましょう。

> The hot, melted rock lava stinks. It smells like rotten eggs. Sometimes, globs of lava fly into the air. They land with a sizzle. The heat melts the ice and snow.

Let's Read! 🔊 1-54

次の文章を読んで、あとの問題に答えましょう。

Winds howl. Snow swirls. Steam rises. You're in Antarctica. You're standing on top of a volcano that's covered in ice. Its name is Mt. Erebus. It's an odd volcano. It never blows its top. Hot lava never runs down its sides.
5 Yet steam rises from its crater.

Look into the crater. Inside you see a lake of lava. The hot, melted rock lava stinks. It smells like rotten eggs. Sometimes, globs of lava fly into the air. They land with a sizzle. The heat melts the ice and snow.

Mt. Erebus

Fire and Ice

10 Mt. Erebus changes all of the land around it. Its steam carves out ice caves. If you crawl inside of one, you'll see ice crystals. They cover the cave walls. Sunlight lights up the ice. It fills the cave with a blue glow.

Outside, icy chimneys rise around you. They're
15 vents that go deep into the Earth. Hot gases and steam rise up through them. The steam hits the cold air, and it freezes into icy towers.

Scientists underneath the blue dome of an ice cave

What Lies Beneath

Mt. Erebus may be icy, but in some ways, it's like other volcanoes. Like them, its heat starts in the
20 Earth's core. The heat rises to the next layer. This is the Earth's rocky mantle. The core's heat melts some of the mantle's rocks. The rocks turn into magma.

The magma rises. It pushes against the Earth's crust. Giant sections of land, called plates, make up the crust. Magma flows through cracks between the plates.
25 When the magma reaches the surface, it becomes lava.

Lava spurts into the air. It falls to the ground and hardens. Over time, layers of lava build a volcano.

Most volcanoes form between the Earth's plates. Mt. Erebus doesn't. Here, the pressure from the magma
30 is too great. It pushes through the crust.

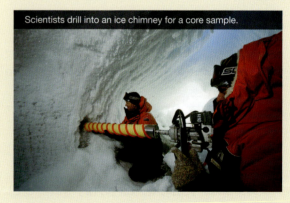
Scientists drill into an ice chimney for a core sample.

Sea Surprise

Mt. Erebus is not the only odd volcano. Scientists have found others in the sea near Antarctica. Until a few years ago, no one knew they were there. Then scientists began making a map of the seafloor. They crisscrossed the area in a boat. They took images of the seafloor.

35 The images surprised the scientists. They showed a line of giant volcanoes rising from the seafloor. Some were really tall. Their tops nearly touched the surface of the sea.

This discovery worried many of the scientists. They knew that with new eruptions, the volcanoes will grow. In time, the volcanoes may grow enough to poke out of the sea.

By now you've learned a few things about volcanoes. Some are very odd. Yet all volcanoes are alike in one way. All of them feel the heat!

NOTES howl「風がヒューヒューうなる」　Mt. Erebus「エレバス山（南極大陸ロス島にある活火山）」　lake of lava「溶岩湖」　glob「しずく」　sizzle「シューシューいう音」　over time「時が経てば」　crisscross「縦横に線を引く、行き来する」　in time「そのうちに」　poke out of the sea「海面から突き出る」

A 本文に関する次の質問に答えましょう。特に指示のない場合は日本語で答えましょう。

Fire and Ice
1. エレバス山の氷の洞穴（氷洞）と氷の煙突（氷塔）はどのようにしてできるでしょうか。

　　氷の洞穴（氷洞）：＿＿＿＿＿＿＿＿＿＿＿＿＿＿＿＿＿＿＿＿＿＿＿＿＿

　　氷の煙突（氷塔）：＿＿＿＿＿＿＿＿＿＿＿＿＿＿＿＿＿＿＿＿＿＿＿＿＿

What Lies Beneath
2. 一般的な火山が噴火する様子の絵を描き、magma、the Earth's crust、lava を示してみましょう。

Sea Surprise
3. 科学者たちは海底に何を見つけたのでしょうか。

4. その結果、科学者たちは何を心配するようになりましたか。

B 写真の説明として、英文が合っていればT、間違っていればFを丸で囲みましょう。Fの場合は訂正しましょう。

1. The tower is made of rock.　　　　　　　　　　　[T / F]
2. It has a hole. Gas and steam rise up through the hole.　[T / F]

C 次の文章は本文の要約です。空所に当てはまる語を記入し、音声を聞いて確認しましょう。
（同じ番号には同じ語が入ります）

Mt. Erebus is a strange volcano in Antarctica. It's an odd volcano. It never blows its top and hot lava never runs down its sides, but the volcano changes all of the land around it. Its steam carves out ice (1.   ) which have ice crystals. Outside are icy (2.   ), which are (3.   ) going deep into the Earth. A giant section of land, which is called a plate, produces the (4.   ). Mt. Erebus doesn't form between the Earth's plates, because the (5.   ) from magma is too much and it pushes through the (4). Scientists took images of the seafloor when they (6.   ) the sea near Antarctica. They were surprised to find a line of giant volcanoes rising from the (7.   ). Some of the tops almost reached the surface of the sea.

Check the Form!

本文に出てきた重要な表現を確認し、あとの問題に答えましょう。

> **〜 enough to ＋動詞の原形**「…するのに十分〜」
>
> enough to 以下は直前の語句（〜）の内容について、それがどの程度なのかを具体的に述べる働きをします。
>
> • In time, the volcanoes may *grow* **enough to poke** out of the sea.

A 意味を考えながら、[　]内の語句を正しく並べ替えましょう。

1. [kind / she / me / was / to / enough / help].
2. [be / enough / hold / would / the door open / kind / you / to]?
3. [I / sensible / am / such a thing / not to / enough / do].

1. _____.

2. _____?

3. _____.

B 1〜3は START の文の赤と青の語句を指定された語句に替えて、4と5は指示に従って、
できるだけ速く言ってみましょう。それができたら、右欄の日本語だけを見て英文が言えるように練習しましょう。また、ペアで練習し、答える人は何も見ずに言えるようにしましょう。

START ▶ He is **strong** enough to **beat** the world champion. （彼は世界王者を負かせるくらい強い。）

1. rich	buy this expensive car	➡ He is rich enough to buy this expensive car.	彼はこの高価な車を買えるくらい金持ちだ。
2. kind	help me	➡ He is kind enough to help me.	彼は私を手伝ってくれるくらい親切だ。
3. clever	do some tricks	➡ He is clever enough to do some tricks.	彼はいくつか芸をするくらい利口だ。
4. 3 の文を Yes/No 疑問文に		➡ Is he clever enough to do some tricks?	彼はいくらか芸をするくらい利口ですか。
5. 4 の疑問文に Yes で答える		➡ Yes, he is.	はい、利口です。

Now Listen to This! 🔊 1-57

音声を聞いて、次の質問に日本語で答えましょう。

1. 南極にあるエレバス山はどうして珍しいのでしょうか。

2. 火山ガスの臭いはどのようなものでしょうか。

3. 南極の周りの海底には何がありますか。

It's Your Turn!

次の質問に対する答えを、〈～ enough to ＋動詞の原形〉を使って完成させましょう。また、ペアで会話してみましょう。

1. How strong was the smell of rotten eggs?
   — _____ turn people away.

2. How hot were the rocks around the old volcano?
   — Even after cooling some, _____ burn holes in my shoes.

3. How much had the new volcano grown?
   — _____ appear out of the sea surface.

Check It Out! 火山ガスのことをインターネットで調べてみましょう。どのようなものが火山から発生し、動植物にどのような影響を与えるでしょうか。（やさしく、わかりやすい説明を探すには、キーワードとして "for kids" を検索窓に入れてみましょう。例：volcanic gases for kids）

UNIT 7 ■ Turn Up the Heat

UNIT 8

Free Fall

Check Your Vocabulary! 1-58〜59

枠内から表の空所に当てはまる日本語や英語を選んで書き入れましょう。また、日本語には品詞も記入しましょう。
（N: 名詞　V: 動詞　Adj: 形容詞　Adv: 副詞）

fall	(N) 落下	save	(V) 救う
record	( )		(V) 膨張する
rubber	( )		(Adj) 普通の
stiff	( )		(Adv) きつく
hate	( )		(N) 秒
rise	( )		(N) 回転　(V) 回転する
atmosphere	( )		(V) 気絶する、卒倒する
less	( )		(V) 戦う
liquid	( )		(N) 恐怖

上がる	嫌う	大気圏	expand	fight	second
液体、水分	記録	より少ない	faint	normal	spin
堅い	ゴム	落下	fear	~~save~~	tightly

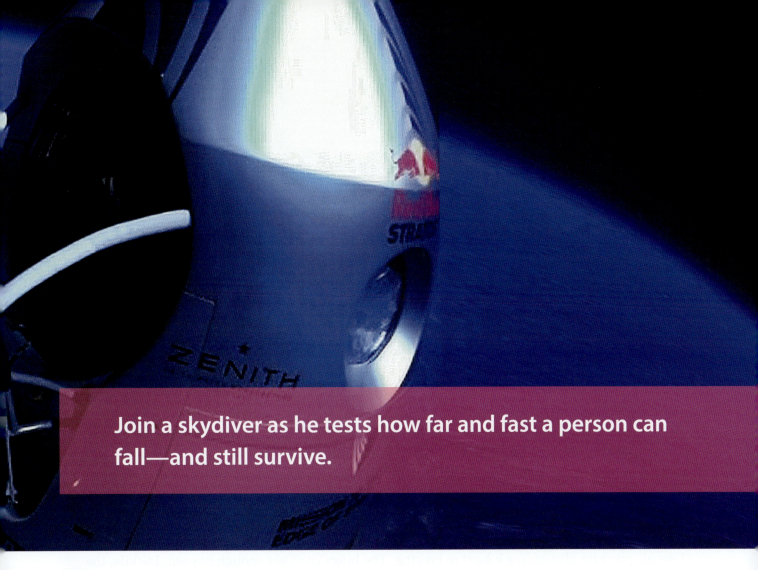

Join a skydiver as he tests how far and fast a person can fall—and still survive.

Listen Up! 1-60

本文に関する音声を聞いて、次の質問に英語で答えましょう。

1. How long has Baumgartner dreamed of this fall?

2. How large could the human body become above the sky?

Read Aloud! 1-61

スカイダイバーが空高く上がったときに人間の体に起こる変化に注意して、次の文章を音読してみましょう。

> There is less air pressure this high up. That does strange things to the human body. Liquids in the body turn into a gas. The gas expands. This causes the body to swell.

UNIT 8 Free Fall

Let's Read! 1-62

次の文章を読んで、あとの問題に答えましょう。

Jumping for Science

Felix Baumgartner has dreamed of this fall for seven years. If all goes well, it will break a record.

The fall could also answer some scientific questions. What will such a long fall do to the human body? Will the special suit made to protect him work?

Only his jump can answer these questions. This information could save lives one day. It could help astronauts who run into trouble high above the Earth.

For now, the skydiver squeezes into his special suit. It's heavy. It stinks of rubber. It's stiff. He can barely move.

He hates the suit. Yet he must wear it. He could never survive the fall without it.

Baumgartner's capsule

Danger in the Air

His balloon is rising into the Earth's upper atmosphere. That's higher than the highest clouds. There is less air pressure this high up. That does strange things to the human body. Liquids in the body turn into a gas. The gas expands. This causes the body to swell. It can swell to two times its normal size.

Breathing Problems

Less air pressure also makes it hard to breathe. The lungs can't get enough oxygen. Luckily, the suit protects the skydiver. It fits his body tightly. That keeps him from swelling up. It also gives him oxygen.

He crawls into a capsule wearing his suit. The capsule is attached to the balloon. The balloon lifts off. Now, he's on his way.

Going Up

The balloon stops rising after two hours. Now, it's 39 km (24 miles) above the ground. The capsule door rolls open, and he steps onto a ledge.

Spinning

About 30 seconds into the fall, the skydiver starts spinning. It looks like he's doing cartwheels. That's not good. If he spins too fast, he could faint.

So he fights the spin. He sticks out one arm. He spins faster. He pulls it back in. He sticks out the other one. He slowly stops spinning.

He falls 1,385 km (844 miles) per hour. It's a speed record! No one has ever gone that fast in a free fall.

Landing

Now, he's closer to the Earth. The air is thicker. He's still falling, but he starts to slow down.

He opens his parachute. The chute catches the air. He floats the rest of the way to the ground and lands safely. Nine minutes and 18 seconds after he jumped, his free fall is over.

He feels great. He pumps his fist in the air. All the planning and fear were worth it. "Adventure," he says, "is how we learn."

NOTES free fall「重力の作用だけの落下、自由落下、落下傘の開く前の落下」 do to the human body「人間の体に影響を与える」 run into trouble「困難に陥る」 squeeze into「(体などを)…に押し込む」 cartwheel「側転」 pump「上下に動かす」

A 本文に関する次の質問に答えましょう。特に指示のない場合は日本語で答えましょう。

Jumping for Science
1. Baumgartner は落下用のスーツを気に入っているでしょうか。また、その理由は何でしょうか。

Danger in the Air
2. 上空では体が膨れるという現象が起こります。それに至る順番に番号を入れましょう。
- body swells [   ]
- liquids in the body turn into a gas [   ]
- less air pressure [1]
- the gas expands [   ]

Breathing Problems
3. 体の膨張を和らげるのに役立つものは何でしょうか。

Spinning
4. 落下の際の急激なスピンはどのような状態を起こすことがあるでしょうか。

Landing
5. Baumgartner はダイビングや冒険についてどのように感じ考えていますか。わかったことを書いてみましょう。

B 次の文章は本文の要約です。空所に当てはまる語を記入し、音声を聞いて確認しましょう。　1-63

Baumgartner is a skydiver who had dreamed of this fall for seven years. He tests how far and fast a person can fall and still (1.   ). There is less air pressure up above the clouds, which causes the human body to (2.   ) to two times its normal size. Less air pressure also makes it difficult to breathe and the (3.   ) cannot get enough oxygen. Fortunately, the special suit (4.   ) the skydiver because it fits his body tightly. It also gives him oxygen. When the skydiver falls, he starts spinning. If he spins too fast, he could (5.   ), so he has to fight the (6.   ). Baumgartner set a speed record falling 1,385 km per hour. His free fall ended 9 minutes and 18 seconds after he jumped.

Check the Form!

本文に出てきた重要な表現を確認し、あとの問題に答えましょう。

> **make it ～ to＋動詞の原形**「…することを～にする」
>
> it は to 以下の内容を指します。
>
> - Less air pressure also **makes it *hard* to breathe**.
>   （より低い気圧は呼吸することを難しくもする。→気圧がより低いので呼吸しにくくもなる。）

A 意味を考えながら、[　] 内の語句を正しく並べ替えましょう。

1. This book [learn / it / to / will make / about skydiving / easier].
2. The Internet [access / it / large amounts of information / easier / has made / to].
3. Noisy cars [it / to / impossible / sleep well / make].

1. This book _____ .

2. The Internet _____ .

3. Noisy cars _____ .

Felix Baumgartner, on hand of giant Jesus statue, is ready to jump.

B 次の会話をペアで練習し、少なくとも▇▇の部分は下の英訳を見ずに言えるようになりましょう。 🔊 1-64

Jane: What's the matter? You look worried.
Tom: I'm having trouble doing my homework for Japanese. Japanese is too difficult for me.
Jane: Then why don't you take a look at this?
　　　1. _____. (この本は日本語をより理解しやすくしてくれるわよ)
Tom: What is this? Oh, this book has many illustrations and pictures.
　　　2. _____. (日本語をより理解しやすくしてくれるだろうね)
　　　Can I borrow it?
Jane: Sure, but please return it by next Monday. I need it for Tuesday's class.
Tom: OK. I will.

> 1. This book will **make it easier to understand** Japanese　　2. It should **make it easier to understand** Japanese

Now Listen to This! 🔊 1-65

音声を聞いて、次の質問に日本語で答えましょう。

1. このスカイダイバーは何をテストしているのでしょうか。
　_____

2. 着ているスーツは具体的にどんな役割をしていますか。
　_____

3. 地上へ帰還するのにどのくらいかかりますか。
　_____

It's Your Turn!

次の質問に、[　]内の語句を使って答えてみましょう。また、ペアで会話してみましょう。

1. What is this book for? [it / make it / to]
　— _____.

2. What is this very small spoon for? [it / make it / to]
　— _____.

3. She tries to study English grammar without a dictionary. What do you think of it? [it / make it / to]
　— _____.

Check It Out! スカイダイビングはスポーツにもなっていますが、その安全性についてインターネットを使い、英語で調べてみましょう。その際、どのようなキーワードで検索したらよいでしょうか。

UNIT 8　Free Fall

UNIT 9

The Hidden Lives of Leaves

Check Your Vocabulary! 2-02~03

枠内から表の空所に当てはまる日本語や英語を選んで書き入れましょう。また、日本語には品詞も記入しましょう。
(N: 名詞　V: 動詞　Adj: 形容詞　Adv: 副詞)

botanist	(N) 植物学者	below	(Adv) より下に
study	(　)		(V) 取り込む、捕える
photosynthesis	(　)		(V) 広げる、広がる
carbon dioxide	(　)		(N) 茎、幹
land	(　)		(N) 模様、柄
miracle	(　)		(V) 失う
rest	(　)		(V) 次第に薄れる
soil	(　)		(V) 現れる
branch	(　)		(V) 死ぬ

枝	研究する	着地する	appear	die	pattern
奇跡	光合成	土	~~below~~	fade	spread
休息する	植物学者	二酸化炭素	capture	lose	stem

58

A tree needs thousands of leaves to keep it alive.
From morning to night, they make food for the tree.

Listen Up! 2-04

本文に関する音声を聞いて、次の質問に英語で答えましょう。

1. What is Mark Olson's job?

2. How does Mark Olson look at tree leaves?

Read Aloud! 2-05

次の文章は、植物が養分を作り出す様子を説明しています。その仕組みを理解しながら、音読してみましょう。

> Plants mix water with carbon dioxide gas. This makes the plant's food. It also makes the oxygen that we breathe.

Let's Read! 2-06

次の文章を読んで、あとの問題に答えましょう。

The trees in the forest are full of sound. Birds squawk and chirp. Monkeys call. Snakes hiss.

Suddenly, there's a buzzing sound. It grows louder. It's a man! He is flying over the trees. A buzzing glider is strapped to his back.

Meet Mark Olson. He's a botanist who studies trees. He's flying over the treetops to look at
5 leaves. He studies tree leaves to see how they use sunlight.

Leaves at Work

Olson knows that leaves use the sun's energy to make food. This is called photosynthesis.

Plants mix water with carbon dioxide gas. This makes
10 the plant's food. It also makes the oxygen that we breathe.

Olson gets ready to land. The glider carries him to the ground. He lands gently near the trees he's been studying. They're called moringa trees.

People use this tree's leaves and roots for food and
15 medicine. Some people call them miracle trees. To Olson, the miracle is what happens inside each leaf.

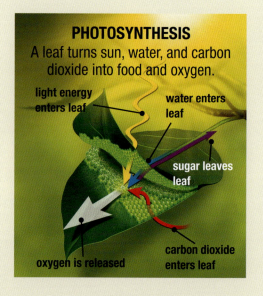

Using Sunlight

At night, most tree leaves rest. At sunrise, the leaves get to work. They open their tiny pores, or holes. Water vapor enters the pores. Carbon dioxide enters, too. Chlorophyll inside the leaves soaks
20 up the sunlight.

Deep in the soil, the roots take in water. The water goes up the trunk. It goes into each branch and leaf. Photosynthesis begins. A tree needs thousands of leaves to keep it alive. From morning to night, they make food for the tree.

Above and Below

25 Olson's glider helps him study leaves. He can see how leaves grow to capture sunlight.

A tree with large leaves has its leaves spread far apart. The extra space lets in more sunlight. A tree with small leaves grows its leaves closer together.

30 Some leaves grow in a spiral around their stems. Others grow across from one another. Many have notched or cutout edges. Light can shine around the cutout parts to reach the leaves below.

Olson knows all the different patterns leaves make. He knows that each pattern helps a tree get as much sunlight as possible.

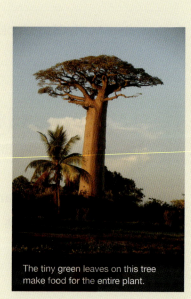

The tiny green leaves on this tree make food for the entire plant.

Life and Death

Many tree leaves make food during spring and summer. Then comes autumn. The days grow shorter. It gets cooler.

In the fall, deciduous trees begin to change. These trees lose their leaves in winter. First, photosynthesis slows down. The strong green of the chlorophyll fades. Now other leaf colors like red, orange, and yellow appear. Finally, the leaves die. In the spring, new leaves will grow.

NOTES squawk「(鳥が) ガーガー鳴く」 chirp「(小鳥や虫が) チーッチーッとさえずる」 hiss「(ヘビなどが) シューと音を出す」 buzz「(蜂などが) ブンブンと飛び回る」 pore「葉の気孔」 water vapor「水蒸気」 chlorophyll「クロロフィル」 soak up「吸い込む、吸収する」 grow in a spiral「らせん状に (くるくる回りながら) 成長する」 notched「V字型の」 deciduous trees「落葉樹」

A 本文に関する次の質問に答えましょう。特に指示のない場合は日本語で答えましょう。

Leaves at Work

1. photosynthesis には何が必要でしょうか。

Using Sunlight

2. 朝になると葉はどのような準備を始めますか。

3. 植物はなぜたくさんの葉が必要なのでしょうか。

Above and Below

4. 紹介されているさまざまな葉の形を描いてみましょう。

Life and Death

5. 秋になったときに葉に起こる変化をまとめてみましょう。

B 次の文章は本文の要約です。空所に当てはまる語を記入し、音声を聞いて確認しましょう。
（同じ番号には同じ語が入ります） 2-07

Mark Olson is a (1.　　　　　). He looks at trees from the air by using a (2.　　　　　). He studies how leaves use (3.　　　　　) to make food. This process of making food is called photosynthesis. Plants make their food from water and (4.　　　　　), and they also emit (5.　　　　　) for us to breathe. Various trees have different types of leaves to help each tree get (3) effectively. When the days become shorter, the colors of deciduous trees change from (6.　　　　　) to red, orange, or yellow. The leaves then die, but in the spring, new leaves grow again.

Check the Form!

本文に出てきた重要な表現を確認し、あとの問題に答えましょう。

> **疑問詞＋S＋V（間接疑問）**
>
> 通常の疑問文と違い、疑問詞の後は肯定文と同じ形になることに注意しましょう。
>
> - He studies tree leaves to see **how they use** sunlight.
> - He can see **how leaves grow** to capture sunlight.

A 意味を考えながら、[　　]内の語句を正しく並べ替えましょう。

1. Just imagine [be like / your life / what / would] without bones. (⇒ Unit 1)
2. He knows [makes / a good photo / what]. (⇒ Unit 10)
3. I learn [formed / space objects / were / when and how]. (⇒ Unit 12)

1. Just imagine _____ without bones.

2. He knows _____.

3. I learn _____.

B **START** の文の赤の語句を1～5の指定された語句に替えて、できるだけ速く言ってみましょう。それができたら、右欄の日本語だけを見て英文が言えるように練習しましょう。また、ペアで練習し、答える人は何も見ずに言えるようにしましょう。 2-08

START Do you know **what she bought** at the supermarket?
（彼女がスーパーで何を買ったか知っていますか。）

1. how he got a perfect score	→ Do you know how he got a perfect score?	彼がどうやって満点を取ったか知っていますか。
2. what kind of fruits he likes	→ Do you know what kind of fruits he likes?	彼がどんな種類の果物を好きか知っていますか。

3. what she said to him	➡ Do you know what she said to him?	彼女が彼に何を言ったか知っていますか。
4. what he said to her	➡ Do you know what he said to her?	彼が彼女に何を言ったか知っていますか。
5. what type of PC I should buy	➡ Do you know what type of PC I should buy?	僕がどんなタイプのパソコンを買うべきかわかりますか。

Now Listen to This! 2-09

音声を聞いて、次の質問に日本語で答えましょう。

1. 光合成の際に植物は何を結合させるでしょうか。

2. glucose とは何でしょうか。

3. chlorophyll はどんな働きをしているでしょうか。

It's Your Turn!

Now Listen to This! で聞いたインタビューを参考にして、自分で何かについて説明してみましょう。以下の空欄を埋めましょう。

説明するもの：＿＿＿＿＿＿＿＿＿＿＿＿＿＿＿＿＿＿＿＿＿＿＿＿＿＿＿

（例：Chlorophyll）

1. What are you going to explain?

— Let me explain ＿＿＿＿＿＿＿＿＿＿＿＿＿＿＿＿＿＿＿＿＿＿＿＿＿.

（例：Let me explain chlorophyll.）

2. What is it / are they?

— ＿＿＿＿＿＿＿＿ is / are ＿＿＿＿＿＿＿＿＿＿＿＿＿＿＿＿＿＿＿＿.

（例：Chlorophyll is the green substance in leaves.）

3. Why is it / are they important?

— It is / They are important because ＿＿＿＿＿＿＿＿＿＿＿＿＿＿＿＿.

（例：It is important because it can use sunlight to change carbon dioxide into oxygen and glucose.）

Check It Out!

1. 本文に出てきた moringa tree について、もっと詳しいことを調べてみましょう。
2. インターネットで Mark Olson に関するいろいろな情報を確認してみましょう。

UNIT 10

Getting the Shot

Check Your Vocabulary! 2-10~11

枠内から表の空所に当てはまる日本語や英語を選んで書き入れましょう。また、日本語には品詞も記入しましょう。
(N: 名詞　V: 動詞　Adj: 形容詞　Adv: 副詞)

spot	(V) 見つける	bite	(V) 噛む
reach	( )		(V) 取り囲む
look for	( )		(Adj) 目に見える
cage	( )		(Adj) 危険な
distance	( )		(Adj) 怖い、恐ろしい
confuse	( )		(Adj) わくわくさせるような
circle	( )		(V) 探検する
curious	( )		(V) 捕える
sting	( )		(V) …に覆われている

おり	困惑させる	手を伸ばす	be covered by	exciting	surround
距離	刺す	~~見つける~~	~~bite~~	explore	trap
好奇心の強い	旋回する	…を探す	dangerous	scary	visible

64

David Doubilet waited beneath the ocean waves in his scuba gear. He was looking for sharks. Doubilet is a photographer for National Geographic.

Listen Up! 2-12

本文に関する音声を聞いて、次の質問に英語で答えましょう。

1. What is David Doubilet's job?

2. What happened when Doubilet was taking pictures of the shark?

Read Aloud! 2-13

次の文章は、上の写真の後の描写です。場面と意味を考えながら、臨場感が出るように音読してみましょう。

He pushed the shark away using his camera. This confused the shark. It gave Doubilet time to get to the cage. His partner pulled him inside.

UNIT 10 Getting the Shot

Let's Read! 2-14

次の文章を読んで、あとの問題に答えましょう。

Doubilet spotted a great white shark. Click. He took a picture. The shark swam closer. Click, click. Now the shark was too close.

Doubilet reached behind him. He was looking for the metal shark cage. The cage's bars would protect him. His dive partner was waiting inside. Yet the cage wasn't there! A wave had pushed it away.

Doubilet scooted closer to the cage. The shark followed. There wasn't much distance between them now. Doubilet had to think fast.

He pushed the shark away using his camera. This confused the shark. It gave Doubilet time to get to the cage. His partner pulled him inside. The shark circled the cage. It was still curious about Doubilet.

Camera Shy

Doubilet knows a lot about cameras and light. He knows what makes a good photo. He also knows about ocean habitats and sea creatures.

It's not easy to take pictures of fish. Most of them don't like to have their picture taken. "Fish want to run away from you," Doubilet says. Many of his photos show the same thing. They show the back ends of fish.

One day, Doubilet got really lucky. He shot one of his favorite pictures. It's a close-up shot of a parrotfish.

The colorful fish was sleeping. He took its photo. He got his camera as close as possible. Then he took a picture of the fish's "perfect smile." Later, the fish woke up. Then the fish showed how it used those teeth. It bit into corals to find food.

Picture 1

Underwater Surprises

Doubilet says the water can be a strange place. It is also full of surprises. Once, he and his partner were in a saltwater lake. Doubilet watched jellyfish surround his partner. Only his partner's head and hand were visible.

Most jellyfish can sting. So swimming in the middle of a lot of them could be dangerous. Yet the jellyfish in this lake could not sting. Swimming among them wasn't scary. It was exciting instead.

Picture 2

Another Dive

Doubilet's travels are not over. He wants to explore many other places. Each of his photos shows a small part of our world. Each one traps a moment in time.

Most of the Earth is covered by water. This gives Doubilet a lot to do. "We're only just beginning," he says. Click. Click. Click.

NOTES click「パシャ（シャッターの音）」 A wave had pushed it away.「波がオリを押し流してしまっていた」 scoot「急いで行く」 habitat「生息地」 creature「生物」 parrotfish「ブダイ科の魚」 coral「サンゴ」 jellyfish「クラゲ」 traps a moment in time「ちょうどよい瞬間をとらえている」

A 本文に関する次の質問に答えましょう。特に指示のない場合は日本語で答えましょう。

1. 次の絵は第4パラグラフまでの内容を示したものです。正しい順序になるよう番号を付けましょう。

(*1*)　　　　(　)　　　　(　)　　　　(　)

Camera Shy

2. 魚の写真を撮るときに難しいのはどのような点でしょうか。
_____

3. Picture 1 は何の写真でしょうか。また、この写真が撮られたとき、被写体は何をしていたでしょうか。
_____

Underwater Surprises

4. 水中での驚いた出来事について、次の語句の意味を使ってまとめてみましょう。
　[saltwater lake / jellyfish / surround his partner / visible / sting / scary / exciting]
_____
_____

Another Dive

5. Doubilet は自分の仕事に関してどのような態度や思いを示しているでしょうか。わかったことを書いてみましょう。
_____
_____

B Picture 2 の写真の描写として英文が正しければT、間違っていればFを丸で囲みましょう。Fの場合は訂正しましょう。

1. David Doubilet is surrounded by jellyfish.　　[T / F]
2. This photo was taken in the sea.　　[T / F]

C 次の文章は本文の要約です。空所に当てはまる語を記入し、音声を聞いて確認しましょう（同じ番号には同じ語が入ります）。

David Doubilet is a marine photographer. He takes pictures of many kinds of marine life such as (1.   ) or (2.   ). He enjoys his career a lot, but sometimes he faces danger. One day he found a big shark under water. However, when he was taking pictures of it, he got too (3.   ) to the shark and was nearly attacked. Another day he took pictures of a fish which looked as if it were (4.   ). He has also taken pictures of many (2) surrounding his (5.   ). He wants to (6.   ) many other places in the world to take more pictures.

Check the Form!

本文に出てきた重要な表現を確認し、あとの問題に答えましょう。

> **have ＋ A（名詞）＋過去分詞** 「Aを…してもらう、…される」
>
> A（名詞）と過去分詞の間には「受け身」の意味関係があります。
>
> - Most of them don't like to **have *their picture* taken**.
>   （彼らのほとんどは、写真を撮られることを好まない。）

A 意味を考えながら、[　　]内の語句を正しく並べ替えましょう。

1. My watch is broken. I have to [it / have / repaired].
2. He [on the train / his bag / had / stolen], so he went to the police box.
3. I will buy this refrigerator. [have / delivered / can / it / I]?

1. My watch is broken. I have to _____.

2. He _____, so he went to the police box.

3. I will buy this refrigerator. _____?

B START ▶ の文の赤と青の語句を1〜4の指定された語句に替えて（青の動詞は過去分詞にする）、できるだけ速く言ってみましょう。それができたら、右欄の日本語だけを見て英文が言えるように練習しましょう。また、ペアで練習し、答える人は何も見ずに言えるようにしましょう。

START ▶ I **had my PC repaired**. （私はパソコンを修理してもらった。）

1. my hair	cut	➡ I had my hair cut.	私は髪を切ってもらった。
2. my blood	examine	➡ I had my blood examined.	私は血液を検査してもらった。
3. my bicycle	steal	➡ I had my bicycle stolen.	私は自転車を盗まれた。
4. my car	damage	➡ I had my car damaged.	私は車を壊された。

Now Listen to This! 2-17

音声を聞いて、次の質問に日本語で答えましょう。

1. 発表者の職業は何でしょうか。
   _____

2. どのような生物が言及されていますか。
   _____

3. 自分の仕事についてどのように言っているでしょうか。
   _____

It's Your Turn!

次の質問に対する自分の答えを完成させましょう。また、ペアで会話してみましょう。

1. What kind of work do you do?
   — I'm _____.
   （例：I'm a photographer.）

2. Can you show me some of your photographs?
   — Here are _____.
   （例：Here are some photos that I took recently. They were taken in Kyoto / at a festival in Osaka.）

3. What do you like best about your work?
   — I like _____.
   （例：I like going to various places and taking photos of interesting things.）

Check It Out! David Doubilet や他の海洋写真家たちの情報（例：写真、プロフィール、活動）をインターネットで探して確認してみましょう。英語のキーワードとして David Doubilet や professional diving、underwater photography などがあります。

UNIT 11

Attack of the Germs

Check Your Vocabulary! 2-18~19

枠内から表の空所に当てはまる日本語や英語を選んで書き入れましょう。また、日本語には品詞も記入しましょう。
（N: 名詞　V: 動詞　Adj: 形容詞　Adv: 副詞）

invader	(N) 侵入者		*immune*	(N) 免疫
germ	( )			(V) 破壊する
pass on	( )			(V) 警告する
bacteria	( )			(N) 化学物質
cell	( )			(V) くしゃみをする
digest	( )			(V) 咳をする
harmful	( )			(N) 白血球
virus	( )			(N) 抗体
cause	( )			(Adv) しばしば

ウイルス	細胞	バクテリア		antibody	destroy	sneeze
うつす	消化する	引き起こす		chemical	~~immune~~	warn
細菌	侵入者	有害な		cough	often	white blood cell

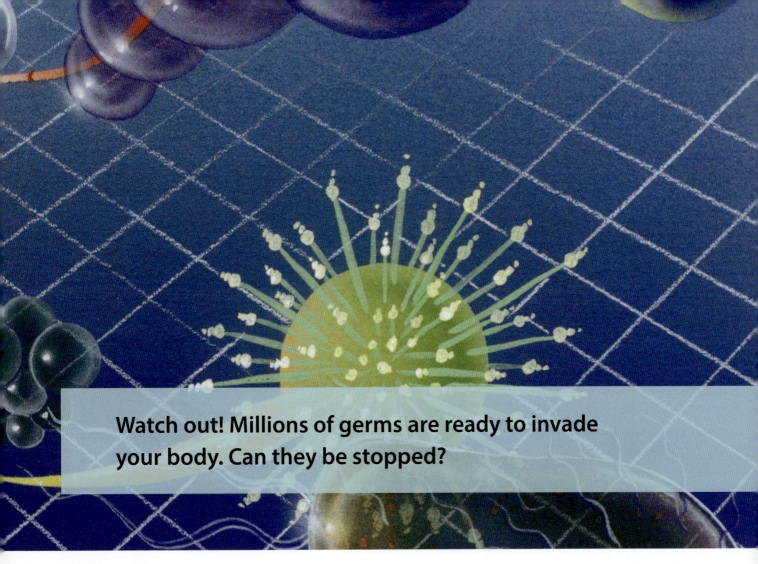

Watch out! Millions of germs are ready to invade your body. Can they be stopped?

Listen Up! 2-20

本文に関する音声を聞いて、次の質問に英語で答えましょう。

1. What can bacteria do to you?

2. Where do viruses live?

Read Aloud! 2-21

細菌のいる場所について理解しながら、次の文章を音読してみましょう。

> Germs are all around you. They're on your skin. Sometimes, they get inside your body. They float in the air you breathe. They ride on the food you eat.

Let's Read! 🔊 2-22

次の文章を読んで、あとの問題に答えましょう。

Meet the Invaders

It starts with germs. Germs are so small, you can't see them. Yet they are trouble. They can make you sick.

Germs are all around you. They're on your skin. Sometimes, they get inside your body. They
5 float in the air you breathe. They ride on the food you eat. Biting insects can infect you with germs.

Sick people may pass on germs, too. Once inside your body, germs make more germs.

Unwanted Guests

Two kinds of germs can harm your body. The first is bacteria. Bacteria are living things made up of only one cell each. Cells are the tiny building
10 blocks of all living things.

Bacteria swim inside your body and can make you sick. Not all bacteria are bad. Some help you digest your food. Some kill the bad bacteria that make you sick.

The other harmful germ is a virus. Viruses live in many places. They
15 live on things you may touch. They may live on people's hands. Viruses can travel through the air. Viruses cause many diseases. They don't swim around in your body. They move into your body's cells.

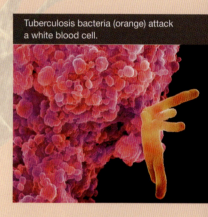

Tuberculosis bacteria (orange) attack a white blood cell.

Fighting Back

Your immune system has tools to destroy germs. Your skin is one of them.
20 It has cells that warn your body when germs attack. Your skin also makes chemicals that kill germs.

Another tool is mucus. Mucus is a thin film of slime. It makes a trap in your nose.

The slimy trap catches germs. Hairs in your nose try to sweep germs
25 out. Coughing or sneezing can toss germs out of your body, too.

The Germ Police

White blood cells float through your blood. They're looking for bacteria and viruses.

Your body makes different kinds of white blood cells. One kind will
30 rush to an open cut. It gobbles up as many germs as it can.

Another kind of white blood cell makes antibodies. Antibodies stop an infection. This kind of blood cell makes antibodies that match only harmful germs. These cells move through your body looking only for those kinds of germs.

35 Once the harmful germs are found, a third kind of blood cell takes over. Some of these cells are fighters. They kill invading viruses. Some of them are like generals. They tell the fighter cells what to do.

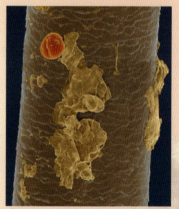

Picture 1

Picture 2

Staying Healthy

Your immune system is working all the time. You can help your immune system do its work. Wash your hands often. Wash them after playing and before eating. Eat healthy foods. Get lots of exercise. Be sure to get a good rest at night. By taking care of your body, you'll feel better. You'll also help your busy immune system.

NOTES mucus「粘液」 toss「振り落とす」 open cut「傷口」 gobble up「食べつくす」 general「将軍、司令官」

A 本文に関する次の質問に答えましょう。特に指示のない場合は日本語で答えましょう。

Meet the Invaders
1. 細菌が見つかる場所を3つ挙げましょう。

   ① _____ ② _____ ③ _____

Unwanted Guests
2. 人間にとって役に立つバクテリアとはどのようなものでしょうか。

   _____

Fighting Back
3. 細菌と戦う免疫機能として挙げられているものを下の語群から選び、丸で囲みましょう。

   | skin medicine mucus nose hairs coughing teeth |

The Germ Police
4. 傷口ができたときの白血球の2種類の働きについて書いてみましょう。

   ① _____
   ② _____

Staying Healthy
5. 細菌と戦うために自分たちでできることは何でしょうか。4つ答えましょう。

   ① _____ ② _____
   ③ _____ ④ _____

B 本文中の写真の説明として英文が正しければT、間違っていればFを丸で囲みましょう。Fの場合は訂正しましょう。

Picture 1: Nose hair catches germs. [T / F]

Picture 2: These red blood cells eat germs. [T / F]

UNIT 11 Attack of the Germs

C 次の文章は本文の要約です。空所に当てはまる語を記入し、音声を聞いて確認しましょう。 2-23

Two kinds of germs can harm your body. The first is bacteria, which are living things made of only one (¹.　　　　　　), the tiny building blocks found in all living things. Bacteria can make you sick but some help you (².　　　　　　) your food. The other harmful germs are (³.　　　　　　) which live in many places such as things you touch and people's hands. They cause many diseases. To fight against those germs, your body has an (⁴.　　　　　　) system. Your skin is one of the tools of the system. Another tool is (⁵.　　　　　　) which is a thin film of slime and makes a trap in your nose. Antibodies are made by one kind of white blood cell and they stop (⁶.　　　　　　). This kind of blood cell produces antibodies that match only harmful germs.

Check the Form!

本文に出てきた重要な表現を確認し、あとの問題に答えましょう。

> **as ~ as S can**「できるだけ~」
>
> 文全体が過去時制のときは、can も過去形の could になります。
>
> - It gobbles up **as many germs as it can**.

A 意味を考えながら、[ ] 内の語句を正しく並べ替えましょう。

1. Read [can / as / as / books / many / you] while you are a student.
2. I swam [as / as / I / fast / could].
3. I want to buy [as / as / expensive / can / I / a car].

1. Read _____ while you are a student.
2. I swam _____.
3. I want to buy _____.

B START の文の赤と青の語句を 1~5 の指定された語句に替えて、できるだけ速く言ってみましょう。それができたら、右欄の日本語だけを見て英文が言えるように練習しましょう。また、ペアで練習し、答える人は何も見ずに言えるようにしましょう。 2-24

A scientist grows bacteria in a lab to study it.

START ▶ Read **as** many books **as you can**. （できるだけ多くの本を読みなさい。）

1. Run	fast	➡ Run as fast as you can.	できるだけ速く走りなさい。
2. Dance	gracefully	➡ Dance as gracefully as you can.	できるだけ優雅に踊りなさい。
3. Come	early	➡ Come as early as you can.	できるだけ早く来なさい。
4. Catch	many fish	➡ Catch as many fish as you can.	できるだけ多くの魚を捕まえなさい。
5. Listen to	many jazz songs	➡ Listen to as many jazz songs as you can.	できるだけ多くのジャズの歌を聴きなさい。

Now Listen to This! 2-25

音声を聞いて、次の質問に日本語で答えましょう。

1. ここで紹介されている病気を引き起こすものとは何でしょうか。

2. 1で答えたものが体に入るのを防いでくれるものは何でしょうか。

3. 体内に病原体が侵入した場合、どのような対抗措置が取られるでしょうか。

It's Your Turn!

次の質問に対する答えを、〈as ～ as you can〉または同様の意味を表す〈as ～ as possible〉を使って完成させましょう。また、ペアで会話してみましょう。

1. How can you strengthen your immune system?
   — We can make it _____ by eating well, exercising and getting a good rest at night.

2. How can you get good results from your experiments?
   — Be _____ when doing the experiments.

3. How can I give a good speech in the contest?
   — Practice _____ in order to give a good speech.

Check It Out! インターネットでバクテリアの画像を検索してみましょう。さまざまな形のものがあります。自分の興味のあるものを選んで、詳しく調べてみましょう。

UNIT 11 ■ Attack of the Germs

UNIT 12

Just Like the Earth?

Check Your Vocabulary! 2-26~27

枠内から表の空所に当てはまる日本語や英語を選んで書き入れましょう。また、日本語には品詞も記入しましょう。
（N: 名詞　V: 動詞　Adj: 形容詞　Adv: 副詞）

result	(N) 結果	compare	(V) 比較する
obey	(　　)		(V) 発見する
remote control	(　　)		(N) 物
solar system	(　　)		(Adj) よく知られた
geology	(　　)		(N) 穴、噴気孔
planet	(　　)		(N) 水星
object	(　　)		(N) がけ、岩壁
fairly	(　　)		(V) 縮む
quickly	(　　)		(N) 10億

遠隔操作	従う	素早く、すぐに	billion	discover	shrink
かなり	太陽系	物、物体	cliff	familiar	stuff
結果	地質学	惑星	~~compare~~	Mercury	vent

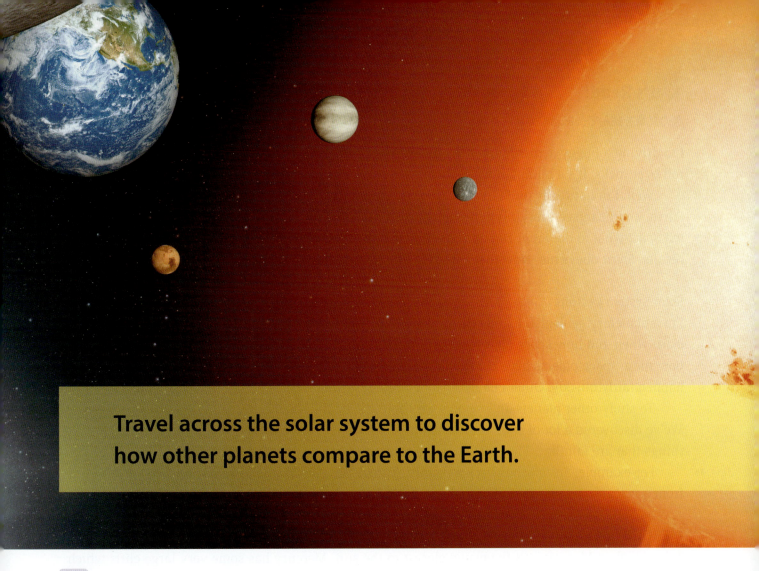

Travel across the solar system to discover how other planets compare to the Earth.

Listen Up!

本文に関する音声を聞いて、次の質問に英語で答えましょう。

1. Who is the author?

2. What does the author learn?

Read Aloud!

火星探査機スピリットが地球に送ってくる画像を理解しながら、次の文章を音読してみましょう。

> *Spirit* sends back a picture. The picture shows an old vent from a volcano. It looks just like vents around volcanoes on the Earth.

Let's Read! 🔊 2-30

次の文章を読んで、あとの問題に答えましょう。

I'm driving a buggy across Mars. It's a rover called *Spirit*. We roll over rocks. It's a bumpy ride.

Well, I'm not really on Mars. But *Spirit* is. I'm on the Earth, and I can see everything through *Spirit's* cameras. I
5 tell *Spirit* what to do: Stop! Dig up some soil. Test it. Send the results. *Spirit* obeys me. Now that's what I call remote control!

The rover *Spirit* explores the surface of Mars.

Solar System Lessons

I'm a planetary geologist. I study the geology of the planets and moons. I learn when and how space objects were formed. One thing that I look at is
10 how these space objects have changed over time. Some kinds of changes happen fairly quickly. Other changes happen really slowly.

To study other planets and moons, we compare them to the Earth. We've discovered a lot of strange stuff in our solar system. We also find things that are familiar. They look just like something we see on the Earth.
15 For example, *Spirit* sends back a picture. The picture shows an old vent from a volcano. It looks just like vents around volcanoes on the Earth.

This crater on Mars is approximately 7 km in diameter and 700 m deep.

MERCURY

Take a look at Mercury. It's the planet closest to the sun. Mercury has some very large cliffs which are faults or large cracks.
20 Mercury's crust isn't made up of plates like the Earth's. Over millions of years, Mercury's core cooled. As it cooled, Mercury slowly shrank. Its hard crust cracked.

The broken pieces moved slowly together. They rode up on top of each other and formed cliffs.

THE EARTH'S MOON

As a kid, I wondered why the Earth's moon has so many dents.
25 Now, I know why. Every dent shows where a space rock suddenly slammed into the moon. *Bam!* Rocks shatter. Some even melt. A huge dent, called a crater, forms.

Smash Hits

Craters don't cover the Earth. There's a reason why. Many space rocks never hit the ground. They burn up quickly when
30 they enter the Earth's atmosphere.

Sometimes, space rocks do strike the Earth. Then they make craters here. Unlike on the moon, though, these craters don't last forever. Wind and rain pound the crater.

This pounding slowly breaks rocks into smaller pieces.
35 This process is called weathering. Then wind, water, and

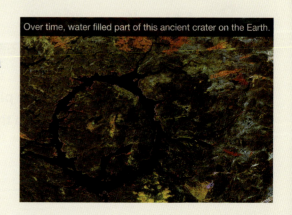
Over time, water filled part of this ancient crater on the Earth.

gravity carry the pieces away. This process is called erosion.

The moon has no atmosphere. So weathering and erosion don't happen there. When a meteorite hits the moon, it forms a crater which may last a long time. More meteorites crash down, too. Today, as many as half a billion craters cover the moon.

40 We have learned that these worlds all have something in common. Just like on the Earth, some changes in space happen quickly, others more slowly.

NOTES buggy「荒地や砂地を走るための自動車」 rover「探査車」 bumpy「ガタガタ揺れる」 fault「断層」 crack「割れ目、亀裂」 atmosphere「大気、大気圏」 pound「何回も強く打つ」 weathering「風化」 erosion「浸食」

A 本文に関する次の質問に日本語で答えましょう。

Solar System Lessons
1. 筆者は月や惑星のどのようなことを調査しているでしょうか。

2. 調査からわかったことはどのようなことでしょうか。

MERCURY
3. 水星のがけ（岩壁）はどのようにして形成されたでしょうか。それは地球の場合と似ているでしょうか。

THE EARTH'S MOON
4. 月のクレーターはどのようにして形成されたのでしょうか。

Smash Hits
5. 地球がクレーターだらけでない理由は何でしょうか。

B クレーターに関する説明として英文が正しければT、間違っていればFを丸で囲みましょう。Fの場合は訂正しましょう。

1. Craters on the moon disappear soon.　　[T / F]
2. A large number of craters cover the moon.　　[T / F]

C 次の文章は本文の要約です。空所に当てはまる語を記入し、音声を聞いて確認しましょう（同じ番号には同じ語が入ります）。 2-31

I'm a planetary (¹.   ). I study when and how space objects were formed. We have discovered many odd things in our solar system and have also found some (².   ) between the planets and the Earth. For example, a rover called *Spirit* sends us a picture showing an old (³.   ) from a volcano which looks like those found on the Earth. Now I know the Earth's moon has so many (⁴.   ) because every dent shows where a space rock suddenly (⁵.   ) into the moon to form a crater. Craters don't cover the Earth because wind and rain (⁶.   ) the crater away. This slowly breaks rocks into small pieces. This process is called weathering. Wind, water, and (⁷.   ) wash away the pieces. This is called erosion.

Check the Form!

本文に出てきた重要な表現を確認し、あとの問題に答えましょう。

> **名詞＋分詞句／形容詞句／前置詞句**
>
> 分詞・形容詞・前置詞は、他の語句と一緒になって名詞の直後に置かれ、大きな名詞句を作ることができます。
>
> - I'm driving a buggy across Mars. It's **a rover called *Spirit***.
> - It's **the planet closest to the sun**.
> - **Some changes in space** happen quickly, others more slowly.

A 意味を考えながら、[　　]内の語句を正しく並べ替えましょう。

1. Bacteria are [only one cell each / made up / living things / of]. (⇒ Unit 11)
2. How far is it to [the planet / the Earth / from / farthest]?
3. [in / can be / the rain forest / meal time] a challenge. (⇒ Unit 6)

1. Bacteria are _____.

2. How far is it to _____?

3. _____ a challenge.

80

B 次の会話を　　で示した大きな名詞句に注意しながらペアで練習し、少なくとも　　の部分は下の英訳を見ずに言えるようになりましょう。 🔊 2-32

Ken: Do you know ¹.　　　　　　　　　　？（地球に一番近い惑星）
Lucy: Maybe Venus or Mars?
Ken: It's Venus.
Lucy: Is Venus ².　　　　　　　　　　？（「宵の明星」や「明けの明星」と呼ばれる惑星）
Ken: Exactly. Venus is a very hot planet. The temperature of its surface is about 500°C. This is because ³.　　　　　　　　　. （大気中のたくさんの二酸化炭素が温室効果を引き起こす）
Lucy: Its environment is quite different ⁴.　　　　　　　. （地球に近い惑星なのに）

1. **the planet nearest to the Earth**   2. **the planet called the Evening Star or the Morning Star**
3. **a lot of carbon dioxide in its atmosphere** causes a greenhouse effect   4. though it is **a planet close to the Earth**

Now Listen to This! 🔊 2-33

音声を聞いて、次の質問に日本語で答えましょう。

1. 遠い惑星のことを観察するにはどうしたらよいでしょうか。

2. 観察結果はどのようにして分析されるでしょうか。

3. もし地球に隕石が衝突してクレーターが形成されたらどうなりますか。

It's Your Turn!

次の質問に、（　）内の語句を使って答えてみましょう。また、ペアで会話してみましょう。

1. What is Venus? (the planet nearest to the Earth)
   —　　　　　　　　　　　　　　　　　　　　　　.

2. Which person is the captain of your team? (the boy wearing an armband)
   —　　　　　　　　　　　　　　　　　　　　　　.

3. Which is the new dress you designed? (the dress in …)
   —　　　　　　　　　　　　　　　　　　　　　　.

Check It Out! NASAの公式ウェブサイト（http://www.nasa.gov/）にアクセスして、興味のある映像を何回か視聴し、理解してみましょう。

UNIT 13

The Skin You're In

Check Your Vocabulary! 2-34~35

枠内から表の空所に当てはまる日本語や英語を選んで書き入れましょう。また、日本語には品詞も記入しましょう。
(N: 名詞　V: 動詞　Adj: 形容詞　Adv: 副詞)

armor	(N) よろい	blood vessel	(N) 血管
temperature	(　)		(V) 山積みにする
tough	(　)		(N) 脳
layer	(　)		(N) 感覚
blow	(　)		(N) 救助
live	(　)		(N) けが
hurt	(　)		(V) 流れる (N) 流れ
bleed	(　)		(N) 汗
nerve	(　)		(Adj) 余分の

生きている	出血する	層	~~blood vessel~~	flow	rescue
痛む	丈夫な	体温	brain	injury	sensation
強風	神経	~~よろい~~	extra	load	sweat

82

The largest organ in your body is the one you wear. Take a look at it.

Listen Up! 2-36

本文に関する音声を聞いて、次の質問に英語で答えましょう。

1. What is the top layer of skin made of?

2. What is the second layer called?

Read Aloud! 2-37

次の文章は、皮膚が傷ついたときの体内の働きを説明しています。その過程や状況を理解しながら、音読してみましょう。

First, the skin around the injury swells. It gets red. That's a sign your body is fighting the germs. Next, blood moves through your body to the place where you were cut. Then, special cells in your blood attack the germs.

Let's Read! 🔊 2-38

次の文章を読んで、あとの問題に答えましょう。

Your skin is like a suit of armor. It isn't hard and shiny. Yet it protects your body. It keeps your body at the same temperature. It lets you feel what you touch.

Let's explore skin from the outside in.

A Tough Outer Layer

5 Skin is an organ made of different layers. An organ is a part of your body that has a job to do. Each layer of skin protects you in different ways.

The top layer is the epidermis. It's made of cells. A cell is the smallest part of a plant or animal.

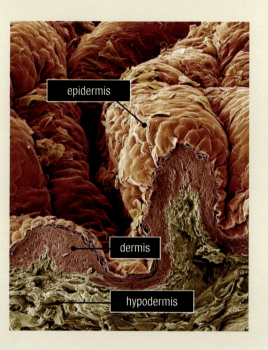

Dead Cells

10 All the cells that make up your outer skin are dead. Yet you couldn't live without them. They block out water, dust, chemicals, and germs. So these harmful things can't get inside your body. They protect you from the sun. They
15 protect you from hard blows.

Skin Cell Factory

The bottom of the epidermis is a skin factory. Live cells are made there. The live cells slowly push to the top of the epidermis. Then they die.

Keep in Touch

20 Now here's something that the epidermis doesn't do.

If you cut or scrape it, it won't hurt or bleed. It can't. It has no nerves or blood vessels. The next layer of skin does, though.

You can thank the nerves in your dermis for your sense of touch.

Sending Signals

25 The dermis is loaded with nerves. The nerves send signals to your brain. You feel sensations faster than the blink of an eye.

Blood to the Rescue

Germs can enter your body when a cut starts bleeding. Your body needs to fight off the germs.

First, the skin around the injury swells. It gets red. That's a sign your body is fighting the
30 germs. Next, blood moves through your body to the place where you were cut. Then, special cells in your blood attack the germs. Some of the cells gobble up the germs. Other cells punch holes in the germs.

Blood vessels work with your skin in other ways, too. If you get too hot, blood vessels get wider. This lets more blood flow and gives off heat. Then you feel sweat on your skin.

A thick layer of blubber helps keep this seal warm.

35　　　Blood vessels shrink if you get too cold. The flow of blood slows down. More heat stays in your body.

Extra Padding

40　The last layer of skin is under the dermis. It's your hypodermis. The hypodermis is like a fatty cushion. It protects the organs inside your body. It also protects you from all the little bumps and bruises your body takes every day.

A Tool to Breathe

Some animals have a special use for their skin. Frogs breathe through their skin.

45　　　You can't use your skin to breathe. Yet skin protects you. It controls your temperature. It helps you feel things. We owe a lot to the skin we're in.

NOTES　epidermis「表皮」　keep in touch「緊密な連絡を保つ」　scrape「すりむく」　dermis「真皮」　blink of an eye「瞬き」
gobble up「…を食べ尽くす」　hypodermis「皮下組織」

A 本文に関する次の質問に答えましょう。特に指示のない場合は日本語で答えましょう。

A Tough Outer Layer, Dead Cells, Skin Cell Factory, Keep in Touch

1. epidermis に関係するものに E を、dermis に関係するものに D を記入しましょう。

(　) Outer cells are dead.　　(　) Protect you from the sun.　　(　) The top layer

(　) The second layer　　(　) It has blood vessels.　　(　) No nerves

Sending Signals

2. 私たちは痛みをどのようにして感じるのでしょうか。[　　]内の語句を並べ替えて、答えとなる英文を作ってみましょう。[signals / your brain / to / send / the nerves]

Blood to the Rescue

3. 皮膚と血液は傷口から細菌が入ったとき、どのようにして戦うのか示してみましょう。

Extra Padding

4. hypodermis はどのような役割をしているのでしょうか。

B 本文の皮膚の写真の説明として英文が正しければT、間違っていればFを丸で囲みましょう。Fの場合は訂正しましょう。

1. The top layer is called the dermis.　　[T / F]

2. The cells of outer skin are alive.　　[T / F]

C 次の文章は本文の要約です。空所に当てはまる語を記入し、音声を聞いて確認しましょう。
（同じ番号には同じ語が入ります） 🔊 2-39

Skin is an (¹.   ) made of different layers. Each layer of skin protects you in many ways. The top layer is the epidermis which is made of cells. Though all the cells making up your outer skin are dead, they block out water, dust, (².   ), and germs. The next layer of skin, which is called the dermis, has (³.   ) for your sense of touch. Blood vessels get wider if you get too hot, letting more blood (⁴.   ) to give off heat. If you get too cold, blood vessels (⁵.   ) and the (4) of blood slows down to make more heat stay in your body. The last layer of your skin under the dermis is your hypodermis which is like a (⁶.   ) cushion. It protects the organs inside your body and also protects you from bumps and bruises.

Check the Form!

本文に出てきた重要な表現を確認し、あとの問題に答えましょう。

> **some ... other(s) ～**「…する人［物］もあれば、～する人［物］もある」
>
> 他の人［物］もあることを暗に示します。例えば、次の文では、細菌を食べてしまったり、穴を開けたりする以外のこと（例：「溶かしてしまう」など）をする細胞がいる可能性があります。
>
> • **Some** of the cells gobble up the germs. **Other** cells punch holes in the germs.
> （細菌を食べてしまう細胞もあれば、細菌に穴を開けてしまう細胞もある。）

A 次の英文を読んで、質問に日本語で答え、英文の意味を書きましょう。

1. Seahorses swim in many oceans of the world. Some are as small as a bean. Others are as big as a banana. (⇒ Unit 3)
   Q: 他にどんな大きさの seahorses がいる可能性があるでしょうか。
   A: _____
   英文の意味: _____

2. Just like on the Earth, some changes in space happen quickly, others more slowly. (⇒ Unit 12)
   Q: 他にどんな変化の度合いが存在する可能性があるでしょうか。
   A: _____
   英文の意味: _____

B **START** の文の赤・青・緑の語句を1～4の指定された語句に替えて、できるだけ速く言ってみましょう。それができたら、右欄の日本語だけを見て英文が言えるように練習しましょう。
また、ペアで練習し、答える人は何も見ずに言えるようにしましょう。

START Some people play baseball, others (play) soccer. （野球をする人もいれば、サッカーをする人もいる。）

1. students	like basketball	tennis	→	Some students like basketball, others (like) tennis.	バスケットボールが好きな学生もいればテニスが好きな学生もいる。
2. members	agree with me	disagree	→	Some members agree with me, others disagree.	私に賛同してくれるメンバーもいれば、賛同しないメンバーもいる。
3. reptiles	swim well	don't	→	Some reptiles swim well, others don't.	うまく泳ぐ爬虫類もいれば、そうでない爬虫類もいる。
4. birds	fly in the sky	run on the ground	→	Some birds fly in the sky, others run on the ground.	空を飛ぶ鳥もいれば、地面を走る鳥もいる。

Now Listen to This! 🔊 2-41

音声を聞いて、次の質問に日本語で答えましょう。

1. 皮膚はどんな役割を果たしているでしょうか。
   _____

2. 新しい皮膚細胞はどこで作られるでしょうか。
   _____

3. 最も内側の皮膚層はどんな役割をしているでしょうか。
   _____

It's Your Turn!

次の質問に、some と other を使って答えてみましょう。また、ペアで会話してみましょう。

1. What do you think of the student reports?
   — _____.

2. Are all of dishes very spicy?
   — _____.

3. Did you enjoy the new movies that you saw last year?
   — _____.

Check It Out!　ウェブサイトで皮膚について説明してある部分を探して、読んだり聞いたりしてみましょう。

UNIT 14

Travel the world to see how powerful forces shape the Earth'

Weirdest Wonders

Check Your Vocabulary! 2-42~43

枠内から表の空所に当てはまる日本語や英語を選んで書き入れましょう。また、日本語には品詞も記入しましょう。
（N: 名詞　V: 動詞　Adj: 形容詞　Adv: 副詞）

crack	(V)割れる (N)割れ目	blast	(V)激しく当たる
valley	( )		(N)小川
pillar	( )		(N)洪水
landform	( )		(N)浸食
force	( )		(N)重さ
pound	( )		(N)風化
tide	( )		(N)酸
million	( )		(N)少し
eventually	( )		(N)鉱物

粉々にする	力	柱	acid	erosion	stream
最終的に	地形	100万	bit	flood	weathering
谷	潮の満ち引き	割れる、割れ目	blast	mineral	weight

88

Listen Up! 2-44

本文に関する音声を聞いて、次の質問に英語で答えましょう。

1. Where can you find the Giant's Causeway?

2. What happened as the lava cooled?

Read Aloud! 2-45

オーストラリアの奇岩がつくられる過程を想像しながら、次の文章を音読してみましょう。

> Long ago, magma pushed up from inside the Earth in Australia. It had collected in a pool under the ground. Then the magma cooled into a giant slab of rock called granite.

Let's Read! 🔊 2-46

次の文章を読んで、あとの問題に答えましょう。

A Giant's Stepping Stones

Long ago, the ground cracked open. Hot lava flowed across the ground. It covered everything in its path.

The lava filled a valley. It formed a large lake. Finally,
5　the lava cooled. As it cooled, it turned hard. Then, crack!

Small cracks appeared in the rock. Many cracks were deep. They formed pillars. The pillars looked like a giant's stepping stones.

This landform is called the Giant's Causeway. It's in Northern Ireland. About 40,000 pillars still stand.

10　Powerful forces wear away the stones. Waves pound the stones. Winds blast them. Tides and gravity tug at them. In time, these forces will change the pillars.

Another million years may go by. Eventually, one by one, the pillars will tumble. The rocks will crumble into pieces. Someday, the Giant's Causeway will disappear.

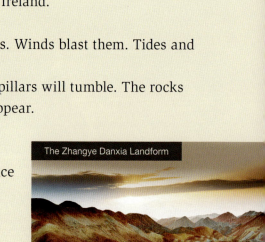
The Giant's Causeway

Rainbow Rocks

15　Rain pounds the ground. Streams turn into raging rivers. Floods race through a valley in ancient China.

Water isn't the only thing on the move here. So are sand, dirt, and rocks. As the water rushes over them, it picks them up.

The water swirls specks of sand and mud. It tumbles pebbles.
20　It pushes big boulders. This movement is called erosion. The water slows. Some of the sand, mud, and rocks settle on the bottom of lakes.

The weight of sand and rocks presses down. Over time, this pressure glues the pieces together. They turn into layers of new rock.

25　At first, these layers are hidden. Then chunks of the Earth's crust shift. Some of the crust rises. It pushes the layers upward. They form mountains.

Rain, ice, and wind change these mountains. They break the rocks into smaller pieces. This is called weathering. What's left today are wavy, colorful hills.

The Zhangye Danxia Landform

Catch a Wave

30　Long ago, magma pushed up from inside the Earth in Australia. It had collected in a pool under the ground. Then the magma cooled into a giant slab of rock called granite.

At first, this rock was buried. Yet even under the ground, it began to weather. Water seeped through the soil. Acids and salts in the water ate away
35　at the rock. They weakened parts of the granite mound.

On the surface, a river formed. The water dug into the land. It picked up and carried away dirt and rock.

Wave Rock

Bit by bit, this erosion uncovered the granite. As more and more land was carried away, the rock seemed to grow taller. Minerals in the water streaked it red and gray. Today it looks like a
40 giant stone wave.

Weathering and erosion are powerful forces. These two forces keep changing the land. They create some of the weirdest places on the Earth.

> **NOTES** stepping stones「飛び石、踏み石」 Giant's Causeway「ジャイアンツコーズウエイ（北アイルランドにある火山活動で生まれた石柱群）」 wear away「すり減らす」 tug at「引っ張る」 granite「花崗岩、御影石」

A 本文に関する次の質問に答えましょう。特に指示のない場合は日本語で答えましょう。

A Giant's Stepping Stones

1. Giant's Causeway が形成された順番に番号を入れましょう。
   (　) 溶岩湖が形成された。
   (　) 溶岩が冷えて割れた。
   (　) 地面が割れ、溶岩が吹き出した。
   (　) 溶岩が谷に流れ込んだ。
   (　) 割れ目が深くなり、柱状になった。

2. Giant's Causeway は100万年後どうなっているでしょうか。また、それはなぜでしょうか。

Rainbow Rocks

3. 雨が川となり運び去るものを、以下の中から選んで丸で囲み、それらを英語に直しましょう。
   水（　　　）　砂（　　　）　柱（　　　）
   岩（　　　）　泥（　　　）　波（　　　）

Catch a Wave

4. オーストラリアの stone wave が形成された順番に番号を入れましょう。
   (　) 冷えたマグマが花崗岩になり、土に埋まっていた。
   (　) 川底が削られ、川の下にあった花崗岩が姿を現し、鉱物によって赤や灰色の縞模様ができた。
   (　) 地中にしみ込んだ水分中の酸と塩分により花崗岩の一部が侵食され弱くなった。
   (　) 一方で地上に川ができたために、川底の泥や石を流していった。

B 本文中の Giant's Causeway の写真の説明として英文が正しければT、間違っていればFを丸で囲みましょう。Fの場合は訂正しましょう。

1. The Giant's Causeway is made up of several pillars.　[T / F]
2. Waves and winds may change the landform.　[T / F]

C 次の文章は本文の要約です。空所に当てはまる語を記入し、音声を聞いて確認しましょう。 2-47

There is an odd landform called the Giant's Causeway in Northern Ireland. After hot (¹.   ) flowed from the ground cracks, it formed a large lake. As it cooled, it turned (².   ) and cracked, which eventually formed pillars which looked like a giant's stepping stones. In (³.   ) China, floods ran through a valley, picking up sand, (⁴.   ), and rocks. The water swirls small pieces of sand and mud, and it (⁵.   ) pebbles. This movement is called erosion. In Australia, the erosion process uncovered the (⁶.   ). Erosion and (⁷.   ) are the powerful forces that keep changing the land.

Check the Form!

本文に出てきた重要な表現を確認し、あとの問題に答えましょう。

> **As ..., ~** 「…(する)につれて、~」「…のとき、~」
>
> as には、when(…するとき)や if(…ならば)などと同様に、文と文をつないで1つの文にする「接続詞」の用法があります。
>
> - **As** it cooled, it turned hard.
> - **As** the water rushes over them, it picks them up.
> - **As** more and more land was carried away, the rock seemed to grow taller.

A 意味を考えながら、[ ]内の語句を正しく並べ替えましょう。

1. [grew / as / darker / it], [colder / it / became].
2. [you / grow / as], [grow and change / bones / your].
3. [more water / as / drank / he], [got / the patient / better].

1. _____.
2. _____.
3. _____.

B START ▶ の文の赤と青の語句を1〜4の指定された語句に替えて、できるだけ速く言ってみましょう。それができたら、右欄の日本語だけを見て英文が言えるように練習しましょう。また、ペアで練習し、答える人は何も見ずに言えるようにしましょう。 2-48

START As I read the book, I came to know more about the skin.
（その本を読むにつれて、私は肌についてより多くを知るようになった。）

1. knew more about him	came to like him	→ As I knew more about him, I came to like him.	彼についてより知るにつれて、私は彼のことを気に入った。
2. studied harder	felt that using English became easier	→ As I studied harder, I felt that using English became easier.	より熱心に勉強するにつれて、私は英語を使うことがもっと簡単になると感じた。
3. grew older	depended less on my parents	→ As I grew older, I depended less on my parents.	成長するにつれて、私は親に頼らなくなった。
4. listened to English songs more	understood them better	→ As I listened to English songs more, I understood them better.	英語の歌をもっと聴くにつれて、私はそれらをより深く理解した。

Now Listen to This! 2-49

音声を聞いて、次の質問に日本語で答えましょう。

1. どこにある地形の話でしょうか。

2. どこの地形と比較しているでしょうか。

3. 溶岩はどこから流れて来たのでしょうか。

It's Your Turn!

次の質問に、as を使って答えてみましょう。また、ペアで会話してみましょう。

1. Why do the rocks look like columns?
   ― _____.

2. Why is the valley so deep?
   ― _____.

3. Why was he able to win the race this year?
   ― _____.

Check It Out! Giant's Causeway のような地形が火星にも見つかっています。インターネットを使い、basalt columns というキーワードで他の地域のものを探してみましょう。

UNIT 14 ■ Weirdest Wonders

UNIT 15

Aquarius

Check Your Vocabulary! 2-50~51

枠内から表の空所に当てはまる日本語や英語を選んで書き入れましょう。また、日本語には品詞も記入しましょう。
（N: 名詞　V: 動詞　Adj: 形容詞　Adv: 副詞）

mission	（ N ）任務	aquanaut	（N）潜水作業員
reef	（　）		（N）調査
conservation	（　）		（Adv）水中で（Adj）水中の
metal	（　）		（N）現場
alga［複 algae］	（　）		（V）つなぐ
lab（laboratory）	（　）		（V）導く
enter	（　）		（V）追う
row	（　）		（Adj）つるつる滑る
tool	（　）		（V）入れておく

岩礁	道具	保護	aquanaut	hold	site
金属製の	任務	藻	chase	lead	slippery
実験室	入る	横列、並び	connect	research	underwater

94

Dive down to the world's only undersea lab.

Listen Up! 2-52

本文に関する音声を聞いて、次の質問に英語で答えましょう。

1. What is *Aquarius*?

2. What is the goal of the program?

Read Aloud! 2-53

次の文章は、海中研究所の内部の様子を説明しています。各部屋の位置を理解しながら、音読してみましょう。

> You see two rows of bunk beds at the far end. You'll sleep in one of them. Next, you see the kitchen. Beyond it is the science lab. That's where you'll keep your tools.

Let's Read! 🔊 2-54

次の文章を読んで、あとの問題に答えましょう。

A school of fish swims around *Aquarius*.

Diving In

You're on a mission to find out how some fish help coral reefs. This work is part of a reef conservation program. The goal of this program is to keep reefs healthy.

5 　　You swim down in the water. Soon, you see something on the ocean floor. It's metal and as big as a school bus.

　　Brain corals and sea sponges grow on its sides. Small fish swim around it. They're eating algae. A small reef shark swims by.

　　This is your first look at *Aquarius*. It's a lab in the ocean. You'll live here for the next 10 days.

10 ### Entering the Lab

You and your partner swim through an opening. Inside, there is a ledge to climb onto.

　　You can't go into the lab right away. First, you need to wash the salt water off your skin. This will keep the lab clean. Then you put on dry clothes. It's safe to go into the lab now.

Getting Settled

15 You look around the lab. You see two rows of bunk beds at the far end. You'll sleep in one of them.

　　Next, you see the kitchen. Beyond it is the science lab. That's where you'll keep your tools. Your work starts in the morning.

An Exciting Excursion

You wake up ready for action. Today you are an aquanaut. An
20 aquanaut does research underwater. You and your partner will study the algae that grow on the reef. Corals grow better without algae. So you'll also study the fish that eat the algae.

　　It's time to swim to the study site. You and your partner suit up. You grab a spool of rope.

25 ### Getting to the Site

Outside, you connect the end of your rope to *Aquarius*. Your rope will be like an underwater road. It will lead you to and from places on the reef.

Something Fishy

30 The cages are all in place around the corals. You start herding fish into the cages. You chase them with hand nets.

　　It's not an easy job. These fish are slippery. Each cage will hold a different kind of fish. You and your partner put two kinds of fish in the last cage. You want to learn which fish eat the most algae.

35 **Checking Your Work**
You watch the cages and take careful notes for the rest of the week. Before you know it, your 10 days on *Aquarius* are over. A new team of scientists will come to take your place.

NOTES brain coral「脳サンゴ」 sea sponge「海綿」 reef shark (= blacktip reef shark)「ツマグロ」 *Aquarius*「フロリダにある海中研究所」 bunk bed「壁に取り付けられたベッド」 a spool of rope「一巻きのロープ」 herd「(家畜などを) 集める、追いやる」

This buoy floats on the surface. It holds the air and power supply for *Aquarius*.

A 本文に関する次の質問に答えましょう。特に指示のない場合は日本語で答えましょう。

Diving In
1. 海中研究所の主な仕事は何をすることでしょうか。次の中から最も適するものを丸で囲みましょう。

   海水をきれいにすること　　サンゴの保護　　魚の保護

Entering the Lab
2. 海中研究所の中に入る前にすることは何でしょうか。

An Exciting Excursion
3. なぜ藻を食べる魚の研究をするのでしょうか。

Getting to the Site
4. 水中に出て作業員が行うことを、次の語句の意味を使ってまとめてみましょう。

   [connect / rope / *Aquarius* / road / lead / to / from / reef]

Something Fishy
5. 魚をおりへ入れることは簡単でしょうか。それはなぜでしょうか。

B 次の文章は本文の要約です。空所に当てはまる語を記入し、音声を聞いて確認しましょう
（同じ番号には同じ語が入ります）。

Aquarius is an undersea lab which is as big as a school bus. Your work in the lab is part of a (1.   ) program. The goal of the program is to keep (2.   ) healthy. Before you go into the lab, you need to wash the salt water (3.   ) your skin to keep the lab clean. You change into dry clothes. One day you work as an (4.   ) who does research underwater. You and your partner will study the algae which grow on the (2). You'll also study the fish that eat algae. Outside, you start herding the fish into the (5.   ). It's not an easy job as these fish are (6.   ). After your 10 days on the lab, a new team of scientists will come to take your place.

Check the Form!

本文に出てきた重要な表現を確認し、あとの問題に答えましょう。

> **to ＋動詞の原形 [形容詞用法]**
>
> 名詞の直後に置いて、その名詞を修飾したり、その名詞の具体的な内容を表したりする使い方があります。
>
> - You're on a mission **to find out** how some fish help coral reefs.
> - It's time **to swim** to the study site.

A 意味を考えながら、[　　]内の語句を正しく並べ替えましょう。

1. Your immune system has [destroy / tools / to / germs]. (⇒ Unit 11)
2. These astronauts will be [land / to / the first humans / on the Red Planet]!
3. This skydiver has [to / good / worry / reason].

1. Your immune system has _____.
2. These astronauts will be _____!
3. This skydiver has _____.

B 次の会話を ▨ で示した大きな名詞句に注意しながらペアで練習し、少なくとも ▨ の部分は下の英訳を見ずに言えるようになりましょう。 🔊 2-56

Bill: Good morning. It's ¹._____. (スタートする準備ができている時間)
Lucy: OK. ²._____. (私たちがそのジャングルを探索する最初の人間になるのね。)
I'm so excited! But first let me check our equipment.
Bill: Hurry up. ³._____. (ぐずぐずしてる時間はないんだ。)
Lucy: Boots to protect our feet and ankles,
⁴._____, (刺す虫を寄せ付けないためのスプレー)
⁵._____, frog costume ... (カエルを見つけるためのヘッドランプ)
Bill: Frog costume? For what?
Lucy: We must teach people about frogs and the dangers they face.
Bill: Ha! There are no people in the jungle! Leave it and hurry!

> 1. time **to get ready** to start
> 2. We'll be the first people **to explore** the jungle
> 3. We have no time **to lose** / There is no time **to lose**
> 4. spray **to keep** biting bugs away
> 5. headlamps **to spot** frogs

98

Now Listen to This! 2-57

音声を聞いて、次の質問に日本語で答えましょう。

1. インタビューを受けている人はどこで仕事をしていますか。
   _____

2. 1人で仕事をしていますか。
   _____

3. どのような仕事をしているでしょうか。
   _____

It's Your Turn!

次の質問に対する自分の答えを完成させましょう。また、ペアで会話してみましょう。

1. What kind of work do you want to do in the future?
   — I want to work as a(n) _____.

2. In order to do that kind of work, what do you need to do?
   — I need to _____.
   （例：I need to study science. / I need to learn how to use English for business.）

3. What country would you like to visit and what would you like to do there?
   — I would like to visit _____ to _____.

Check It Out!　次の単語を組み合わせてインターネットで検索し、coral reefs のことをもっと調べてみましょう。
[defend, defense, protect, protection, conservation, coral reefs, kids]

UNIT 15　Aquarius

Glossary

このリストには、各ユニットの **Check Your Vocabulary!** で扱っている重要語句と、そのユニットの **Let's Read!** 本文での初出ページを収録しています。正しい用法の習得にも役立てましょう。

A

acid	N	酸	90
active	Adj	活動的な、元気な	18
alga	N	藻	96
alike	Adj	似ている	12
amount	N	量	36
ancient	Adj	古代の	36
Antarctica	N	南極大陸	48
antibody	N	抗体	72
appear	V	現れる	61
aquanaut	N	潜水作業員	96
archaeologist	N	考古学者	18
argue	V	口論する	30
armor	N	よろい	84
astronaut	N	宇宙飛行士	30
atmosphere	N	大気圏	54

B

backbone	N	背骨	12
backward	Adv	後ろへ	12
bacteria	N	バクテリア	72
barely	Adv	かろうじて、なんとか	24
be covered by	V	…に覆われている	66
below	Adv	より下に	60
bend	V	曲げる、曲がる	12
billion	N	10億	79
bit	N	少し	91
bite	V	噛む	66
blast	V	激しく当たる	90
bleed	V	出血する	84
block	V	遮る	30
blood vessel	N	血管	84
blow	V	吹く、吐く	48
blow	N	強風	84
botanist	N	植物学者	60
brain	N	脳	84
branch	N	枝	60
breathe	V	呼吸する	30
broken	Adj	骨折した	18
bug spray	N	虫除けスプレー	42
bury	V	埋める、埋葬する	18

C

cage	N	おり	66
calm	Adj	冷静な	42
camouflage	N	偽装、擬態	24
capture	V	取り込む、捕える	60
carbon dioxide	N	二酸化炭素	60
carefully	Adv	注意深く、入念に	42
cause	V	引き起こす	72
cave	N	洞窟、洞穴	48
cell	N	細胞	72
challenge	N	難題	42
chase	V	追う	96
chemical	N	化学物質	72
circle	V	旋回する	66
cliff	N	がけ、岩壁	78
cockroach	N	ゴキブリ	42
colony	N	居留地	30
compare	V	比較する	78
confuse	V	困惑させる	66
connect	V	つなぐ	96
conservation	N	保護	96
coral	N	サンゴ	24
core	N	中心部、核	48
costume	N	衣装	42
cough	V	咳をする	72
crack	V / N	割れる / 割れ目	90

creature	N 生き物	43
crew	N 乗組員	30
crop	N 作物	36
crystal	N 結晶	48
curious	Adj 好奇心の強い	66

D

dangerous	Adj 危険な	66
deadly	Adj 命にかかわるような	19
destroy	V 破壊する	72
die	V 死ぬ	61
digest	V 消化する	72
disappear	V 消える	24
discover	V 発見する	78
disease	N 病気	18
distance	N 距離	66
dragon	N 竜	24

E

enter	V 入る	96
erosion	N 浸食	90
eruption	N 噴火	49
eventually	Adv 最終的に	90
exciting	Adj わくわくさせるような	66
expand	V 膨張する	54
explore	V 探検する	66
extra	Adj 余分の	85

F

fade	V 次第に薄れる	61
faint	V 気絶する、卒倒する	54
fairly	Adv かなり	78
fall	V 落ちる	48
fall	N 落下	54
familiar	Adj よく知られた	78
farmland	N 農地	36
farther	Adv もっと遠くに	30
fear	N 恐怖	55
feed	V 食べ物を与える	36
fight	V 戦う	54
flat	Adj 平らな	12
flood	N 洪水	90
flow	V 流れる N 流れ	84
force	N 力	90
form	V 形作る	12
forward	Adv 前へ	12
freeze	V 凍る	48
frog	N カエル	42
from side to side	Adv 左右へ	24
fuel	N 燃料	30

G

gear	N 道具	42
geology	N 地質学	78
germ	N 細菌	72
gravity	N 重力	30

H

handle	V 対処する	30
harmful	Adj 有害な	72
hate	V 嫌う	54
hold	V 入れておく	96
hungry	Adj 飢えた	36
hunt	V 狩りをする	18
hurt	V 痛む	84
hut	N 小屋	42

I

icy	Adj 氷の（ような）	48
image	N 画像	18
immune	N 免疫	72
indoor	Adj 室内の	36
injury	N けが	84
invader	N 侵入者	72
invent	V 発明する、創り出す	30

J

joint	N 関節	12

L

lab	N 実験室	96
land	V 着地する	60
landform	N 地形	90
lava	N 溶岩	48

layer	N 層	84
lead	V 導く	96
less	Adj より少ない	54
link	V つなげる	12
liquid	N 液体、水分	54
live	Adj 生きている	84
load	V 山積みにする	84
long-sleeved	Adj 長袖の	42
look for	V …を探す	66
lose	V 失う	61
lower	V 下げる　Adj 下方の	12
lung	N 肺	12

M

Mars	N 火星	30
meal	N 食事	42
melt	V 融ける	48
Mercury	N 水星	78
metal	Adj 金属製の	96
million	N 100万	90
mineral	N 鉱物	91
miracle	N 奇跡	60
mission	N 任務	96
mummy	N ミイラ	18
muscle	N 筋肉	12
mystery	N 謎	18

N

nearly	Adv ほぼ、ほとんど	48
nerve	N 神経	84
normal	Adj 普通の	54
nutrient	N 栄養分	36

O

obey	V 従う	78
object	N 物、物体	78
ocean	N 海洋	24
often	Adv しばしば	73
once	Adv かつて、昔	42
one-way	Adj 片道の	30
organ	N 臓器、器官	12
oxygen	N 酸素	30

P

pass on	V うつす	72
pattern	N 模様、柄	60
pest	N 害虫	36
photosynthesis	N 光合成	60
pillar	N 柱	90
planet	N 惑星	78
poison	N 毒	43
population	N 人口	36
pound	V 粉々にする	90
pressure	N 圧力	48
protect	V 保護する、守る	12

Q

quickly	Adv 素早く、すぐに	78

R

radiation	N 放射線	30
reach	V 手を伸ばす	66
record	N 記録	54
reef	N 岩礁	96
remote control	N 遠隔操作	78
rescue	N 救助	84
research	N 調査	96
reshape	V 作り変える	36
rest	V 休息する	60
result	N 結果	78
rise	V 上がる	54
robber	N 強盗、盗賊	18
row	N 横列、並び	96
rubber	N ゴム	54

S

safe	Adj 安全な	36
save	V 救う	54
scale	N うろこ	24
scary	Adj 怖い、恐ろしい	66
seahorse	N タツノオトシゴ	24
seaweed	N 海藻	24
second	N 秒	54
sensation	N 感覚	84
shrink	V 縮む	78

site	N 現場		96
skull	N 頭がい骨		12
slippery	Adj つるつる滑る		96
sneeze	V くしゃみをする		72
soil	N 土		60
solar system	N 太陽系		78
solution	N 解決法		30
solve	V 解決する		18
spaceship	N 宇宙船		30
spin	N 回転 V 回転する		54
spot	V 見つける		66
spread	V 広げる、広がる		60
spurt	V 噴出する		48
stack	V 積み重ねる		36
steal	V 盗む		18
steam	N 水蒸気		48
stem	N 茎、幹		60
stiff	Adj 堅い		54
sting	V 刺す		66
stink	V 悪臭を放つ		48
stream	N 小川		90
strength	N 強さ、体力		18
stretch	V 広がる		24
struggle	V 苦労する		36
study	V 研究する		60
stuff	N 物		78
suffer from	V （病気）を患う		19
surface	N 表面		48
surround	V 取り囲む		66
survive	V 生き残る		24
sweat	N 汗		84

T

tail	N 尾		24
temperature	N 体温		84
terrace	N 段々畑		36
thick	Adj 厚い、太い		12
thin	Adj 薄い、細い		12
tide	N 潮の満ち引き		90
tighten	V 引き締まる、きつくなる		12
tightly	Adv きつく		54
tiny	Adj ごく小さい		24

tip	N 先、先端		24
tomb	N 墓		18
tool	N 道具		96
tough	Adj 丈夫な		84
toxic	Adj 毒性の、有毒な		43
trap	V 捕える		66
treasure	N 宝物		18
turn	V 変わる、…になる		24
turn	V 回転する		36

U

underwater	Adv 水中で Adj 水中の		96
up and down	Adv 上下に		24

V

valley	N 谷		90
vent	N 穴、噴気孔		78
vertical	Adj 垂直の		36
virus	N ウイルス		72
visible	Adj 目に見える		66
visitor	N 訪問者		42
volcano	N 火山		48

W

warn	V 警告する		72
weak	Adj 弱い		19
weather	N 天気		36
weathering	N 風化		90
weight	N 重さ		90
white blood cell	N 白血球		72
wild	Adj 野生の		42
wrap	V 巻く		24
wrong	Adj 悪い、誤った		30

Z

zoologist	N 動物学者		42

Photo Credits:

front cover: (t) © Jerome Ang Chua Photography/Moment Open, (b) © Chris Hill/National Geographic; 10-11: © Digital Vision./Getty Images; 12: (t) © GoodOlga/iStock/Thinkstock, (b) © KristinaPerlerius/iStock/Thinkstock; 13: © Dung Vo Trung/Sygma/Corbis; 16-17: © J. D. Dallet Therin-Weise/Getty Images; 18: (t) © takepicsforfun/iStock/Thinkstock, (b) © Photos.com/PHOTOS.com/Thinkstock; 19: © Photos.com/PHOTOS.com/Thinkstock; 21: (t) © Ingram Publishing/Thinkstock, (b) © fenkieandreas/iStock/Thinkstock; 22-23: © Georgette Douwma/Getty Images; 24: (t) © fenkieandreas/iStock/Thinkstock, (b) © fly1210/iStock/Thinkstock; 25: © Ingram Publishing/Thinkstock; 26: © Nooneoui/iStock/Thinkstock; 28-29: © Denis Scott/CORBIS; 30: (t) © Ben Cooper/Corbis, (b) © MPI/Getty Images; 31: (t) © NASA/JPL/Cornell/ZUMA/Corbis, (b) © Stocktrek/Mars/Corbis; 32: © CORBIS/Corbis; 34-35: © Peter Cade/Getty Images; 36: © LUHUANFENG/iStock /Thinkstock; 37: (l) © Grigory Fedyukovich/iStock/Thinkstock, (r) © Liang Sen/Xinhua Press/Corbis; 38: © laddawanh/iStock/Thinkstock; 40-41: © David Tipling/Getty Images; 42: © 90406050/Alex Bramwell/iStock/Thinkstock, (t) © John Anderson/iStock/Thinkstock; 43: © Alex Bramwell/iStock/Thinkstock, (t) © JaysonPhotography/iStock/Thinkstock, (b) © LUCY COOKE; 44: (t) © photostio/iStock/Thinkstock, (b) © NMelander/iStock/Thinkstock; 46-47: © George Steinmetz/Corbis; 48: (t to b) © Galen Rowell/Corbis, © George Steinmetz/Corbis, © Carsten Peter/National Geographic/Getty Images; 49: © George Steinmetz/Corbis; 52-53: © AFP=Jiji/www.redbullcontentpool.com /Jay Nemeth; 54: © Serghei Velusceac/Hemera/Thinkstock, (t) © Science Photo Library / Pacific Press Service, (b) AFP=Jiji/www.redbullcontentpool.com; 55: © Serghei Hemera/Thinkstock, (t) AFP=Jiji/www.redbullcontentpool.com/Pedrag Vuckovic, (b) © Rex Features / Pacific Press Service; 56: (t) © Serghei Velusceac/Hemera/Thinkstock, (b) © Lobo Press/Getty Images; 58-59: © vovan13/iStock/Thinkstock; 60: (t) © Science Photo Library/Pacific Press Service, (b) © Jean Mazerand/iStock/Thinkstock; 61: (t) © Claire Takacs/Getty Images; 64-65: © JENNIFER HAYES/National Geographic Creative, 66-67: © Olga Khoroshunova/Hemera/Thinkstock; 66: (t) © DAVID DOUBLIET/National Geographic Creative, (b) © DAVID DOUBLIET/National Geographic Creative; 68: © JayAndersons/iStock/Thinkstock; 70-71: © Science Photo Library/Pacific Press Service; 72-73: © Zoonar RF/Zoonar/Thinkstock; 72: (t to b) © Science Photo Library/Pacific Press Service, © Visuals Unlimited/Pacific Press Service, © Visuals Unlimited/Pacific Press Service; 73: (t) © sirawit99/iStock/Thinkstock; 74: (t) © Zoonar RF/Zoonar/Thinkstock, (b) © AlexRaths/iStock/Thinkstock; 76-77: © Science Photo Library/Pacific Press Service; 78:(t to b) © Science Photo Library/Pacific Press Service, © NASA NASA/Getty Images, © Science Source/Pacific Press Service; 82-83: © Shannon Fagan/Getty Images; 84: © STEVE GSCHMEISSNER/Getty Images; 85: © Tom Brakefield/Stockbyte/Thinkstock; 88-89: © Richard Olsenius/Getty Images; 90: (t) © VisitBritain/Britain on View/Getty Images, © yangphoto/iStock/Thinkstock, © Daniel Haller/iStock/Thinkstock; 94-95: © Mark Conlin/Getty Images; 96-97: © Top Photo Corporation/Top Photo Group/Thinkstock; 96: (t) © Stephen Frink/sf@stephenfrink.com/Corbis, (b) © SCIENCE SOURCE/Getty Images; 97: © Brian Skerry/National Geographic/Getty Images; 99: © adokon/iStock/Thinkstock

---

教師用音声 CD 有り（非売品）

Science Frontiers
—Developing Your English with National Geographic
ナショナルジオグラフィックで始める理系英語

2016 年 3 月 1 日　初版発行
2024 年 1 月 20 日　第 6 刷

編著者	服部圭子、日高俊夫、山下弥生、松田佳奈、野口ジュディー
発行者	松村達生
発行所	センゲージ ラーニング株式会社
	〒 102-0073　東京都千代田区九段北 1-11-11　第 2 フナトビル 5 階
	電話　03-3511-4392
	FAX　03-3511-4391
	e-mail: eltjapan@cengage.com
	copyright © 2016 センゲージ ラーニング株式会社

装　　丁	株式会社クリエーターズユニオン　森村直美
組　　版	有限会社ザイン
本文イラスト	湊　敦子
印刷・製本	株式会社ムレコミュニケーションズ

ISBN 978-4-86312-289-5

もし落丁、乱丁、その他不良品がありましたら、お取り替えいたします。
本書の全部または一部を無断で複写（コピー）することは、著作権法上での例外を除き、禁じられていますのでご注意ください。